Gary Alexander

eGAIA

Growing a peaceful, sustainable Earth through communications

www.fast-print.net/store.php

eGaia, Growing a Peaceful, Sustainable Earth through
Communications (Second Edition)
Copyright © Gary Alexander 2014

First edition published in 2002 in England by Lighthouse Books, Diss, Norfolk, IP21 4BU

Illustrations and cover picture by Beverly Curl, cover by David Alexander, Leonardo Suozo and
Oliver Sylvester-Bradley. Cartoons by Sarah Guthrie, Design by Linda Rodgers

A catalogue record for this book is available from the British Library

ISBN 978-178456-102-4

This edition published 2014 by
FASTPRINT PUBLISHING
Peterborough, England.

TABLE OF CONTENTS

Openings

> The problem is essentially that people don't understand each other or themselves. It's in this area of learning to understand ourselves, and therefore learning to live together, that we are defective in the world. So learning to do that is constructing an adequate model of mankind.
>
> If we are looking for a model of mankind, it has to be a cap that fits; and if it is a cap that fits, then people are going to put it on. That is why the problem is open to solution — a solution in which people's behaviour changes because they become progressively enlightened as to their own nature"
>
> *Professor Michael Hussey*

DEDICATION

This book is dedicated to the late Professor Michael Hussey, for many years my closest friend and mentor. He deserves credit for the deepest ideas and for the fundamental changes in my worldview reflected here. His sudden death in 1990 left a huge hole in my life and in that of many others.

This second edition is also dedicated to the thousands of people in the Transition Network and similar projects, who are my allies and the best hope in a generation of making a difference towards the visions in this book.

ACKNOWLEDGEMENTS

A special thanks to the team of good friends who helped me put together the first and second editions: Beverly Curl, Brian Guthrie,, Sarah Guthrie, Tim Holt-Wilson, Linda Rodgers.

Many people have read and commented on this and earlier attempts at writing this book. Many of the ideas were clarified through their comments and in conversation with them, so special thanks to Godfrey, Howard, Allen, Stephen, Tony, Karen, Madeline and all the others I have forgotten to mention.

PART 1 FROM GLOBAL CANCER TO GLOBAL NERVOUS SYSTEM

1 Preface

This book is a journey we will be taking together – you the reader and me. We'll be exploring lots of ideas and possibilities. Some of these will be far from conventional wisdom, so if we are to stay together, I would at least like to be clear about where we start.

However you have come to this book, I imagine you are likely to be in general sympathy with my starting points.

- *A worry about the natural environment.* You have a strong sense that human activities are reaching the limits of the planet: the climate is changing, the weather is becoming more unstable, the air and seas are polluted, we are destroying natural habitats, plants and animals are going extinct rapidly, and more. These issues have been in the public consciousness since the 1960s, but now are really hitting home. A lot more is understood now than then, but nevertheless it still seems to be getting worse, not better. You find this upsetting and would like to see it change. You do what you can in your daily life, but feel that that is probably not much more than tokenism. To a large extent you feel caught in an unsustainable lifestyle.

- *Worries about the economy, local and global, and where it is going.* It is becoming increasingly unstable. Recessions are continuing, more in some countries than others. A total economic crash, like in the 1930s and affecting the whole world, could happen at any time. Very few people have much job security. This despite the efforts of politicians, central bankers etc to keep it stable and prosperous. And so many people get left out. Even in places where times are good, there are lots of people who are struggling. You may be one of them. Or you may see your children or your friends struggling. As for the really poor people in famine areas or in shanty towns, it is almost too painful to think about. And you probably have a sense of resigned cynicism about all the awful things which are done purely in pursuit of money, whether it is arms and tobacco sales, or the corruption that affects business and politics.

- *A sense of hopeless despair about wars and ethnic cleansing.* Yes, the Cold War has ended and the shadow of a nuclear war between the West and Communism has largely cleared. But new wars keep coming (former Yugoslavia, Iraq, Afghanistan, the 'war on terrorism', the Arab Spring – and what will happen between Iran and Israel?) You feel that so many of the conflicts which are left are just as appalling.

- *Nagging doubts about your government.* You may live in a country with a parliamentary democracy and free elections. But somehow it doesn't feel like 'government by the people and for the people'. All sorts of special interests seem to get in the way. Taxes always seem very high but not for the rich or big companies. Public services are being slashed and the large mass of public employees underpaid. You probably vote against the party you think is worse rather than for a party you genuinely identify with. You are sure this kind of government is better than the old feudal system it replaced, or modern totalitarian equivalents. But you imagine that there could be something much better, much more community-based and with a much more human face.

- *Concern about the decline of relationships and community.* If you haven't been part of a broken family yourself, either as a child or an adult, you are likely to know lots of people who are. You know of the damage it causes to all concerned. You probably know about strong communities from your childhood, or from your parents, or from people who have come from other countries where 'they were poor but cared for each other'. You worry about the effects on so many children of both a broken family and a non-existent community.

This book is for people who would like to see major change in these areas, who want to be clearer as to what is desirable in their place and what kind of change is possible. Perhaps you are looking for change in your life and are exploring ideas which may help in that. Or, you may live someplace where the economy is collapsing and major change is really urgent. You may already be devoting some or much of your time to creating change of this sort, and are interested in another perspective on it. You may simply be keeping a watching brief on what is going on and are interested in a book which tries to make some sense of the larger picture.

OUR DIALOGUE

I try to imagine the people who are reading this book so I know what I can assume as I write. It sometimes seems that it would be easier if this could be more of a dialogue than seems to be possible in a book. I would like to know how much you agree with what I have just assumed about you. Have I got it right? Are there areas I have missed out?

> **You** Well, perhaps it can be a limited sort of dialogue. Yes, you have more or less got me right, but I might not express it in the same way. And what about issues of health and diet? Don't those concern you? Anyway, hello.

> **Me** Well hello. Yes, I'm sure there are lots of other areas which we could explore.

Perhaps the first issue we should look at, before the book starts, is whether or not you are open to the possibility that there might be very dramatic changes for the better over the next few generations, if enough people want it and work for it.

> **You** That's not an easy question to answer. I certainly would like to see dramatic changes for the better, but I tend to be quite cynical, especially about people. This book is already sounding somewhat utopian, and I might take some convincing.

> **Me** What worries me is that you might mean utopian in a dismissive fashion – too good to happen.

The book is very much utopian, in the sense of trying to figure out what kind of a society and what kind of relationship with the Earth would work best for us all, humanity in all its diversity, and the rest of life on Earth. That's the big question.

Can we imagine a society in which human activities preserve and enhance rather than destroy the natural world? And in which all the other issues raised above were at least significantly better, if not fully resolved? What might it be like? What sort of jobs would people do? What kinds of social structures would be needed? What would their relationships with one another be like?

What I am hoping to offer more than anything else is that large-scale picture, and to clarify it as fully as I am able. How do the different problems reinforce each other? To help do that, I will need something to compare the problems with. I will try to imagine some possible futures.

> **You** Are you trying to wriggle out of saying you think these possible futures will actually happen?

> **Me** Let's be clear about that from the beginning. I wouldn't be writing about something I believed couldn't happen. What would be the point? But that's not the same as saying I think it will happen. I don't know and don't believe the future is knowable.
>
> In the 12 years between the first and second editions of this book, the world has come much closer to environmental and economic breakdown but at the same time the starting points for a breakthrough have grown too.

Sometimes I feel very positive about the future and other times I think everything is hopeless. I do think it is very important to look at what is desirable, and to understand what might stop it from happening. The necessary changes might not happen simply because not enough people take them seriously, or because people continue to cling to beliefs about the way society works today, even though it is so dysfunctional.

Where do you stand on this? How open are you to change?

You I have a lot of sympathy for change.

THE MIRACLE QUESTION

My preferred approach to looking at the future is similar to that used by 'solution-focused brief therapists', a school of personal and family therapy that works by exploring the positive in people's lives. They say to their clients 'Imagine that you went to sleep, and while you were asleep, a miracle happened so that all your problems were ended. What would you notice when you woke up? What would be different?' This is a technique to bypass their clients' habitual defences, negativity and preoccupation with what is wrong. It allows them to look at what they really want. The therapist can then ask 'What first steps could you take to make that happen?'

So it is in that spirit that I will be looking at possible futures. What do we really want? And later in the book I'll look at steps in those directions.

You Well that sounds a little better. But anyway, why should I believe you? What is so special about your view of the future? Who are you?

Me I don't want you to believe me. When I find a book I like, it is generally because it has clarified something I was already generally sympathetic towards. I hope you will come to agree with me rather than believe me. The ideas will then be as much yours as mine. And as for who I am, perhaps a potted biography will suggest where these ideas came from and give you a preview of them.

WHO AM I?

I was born in New York City in 1943, in a family of immigrant Romanian-Jewish origin. My family and friends were aware of the troubles and conflicts in the city. There were racial problems between various cultures, and lots of crime. We were very aware of the wars, conflicts and hatreds that had afflicted people in the past and that still left their legacy in our multi-cultural city. In particular, we knew about pogroms, Nazism and the holocaust, and residual anti-Semitism. Some of our grandparents were concentration camp survivors, with numbers tattooed on their arms. We were also aware of slavery, the American Civil War, and the residual racial prejudice around us. As an older child and teenager, it was only natural that I should join in with some of the social and political struggles around me, which were, first, the campaigns for racial integration, and later the anti-war and anti-nuclear weapons movements.

I grew up with liberal American values, and viewed New York accordingly. We enjoyed the many cultures that made up the city. We liked each others' food and would join in the celebrations of each others' holidays. We went to Little Italy for the Festival of San Gennaro, to Chinatown for the Chinese New Year. Each year the line down the centre of Fifth Avenue was painted green for the St Patrick's Day parade. We went to midnight mass on Christmas Eve.

It seemed reasonable and normal that we could all retain the forms of our ancestral cultures but at the same time see ourselves as New Yorkers and Americans with all that implied. It seemed reasonable and normal for different cultures to live mixed in together for the most part without difficulty.

In school, my greatest interests were science and mathematics. This led me into an undergraduate degree in electronic engineering from Columbia University. Later I did a Master's degree and then a PhD at Purdue University in Indiana, doing research into non-linear circuit theory. The research was virtually pure mathematics and highly abstract, but it gave me very useful ways of thinking about the dynamic behaviour of complex systems – a set of mental tools which underpins the social views in this

10

book: How feedback processes can create either stability or instability. How systems may have characteristic ways of behaving which involve 'flipping' from one somewhat stable pattern to a quite different one when a tipping point is reached. For example, consider the sudden collapse of Communism in Eastern Europe in 1989 or the Arab Spring, and thus how a major cultural change could follow now from our economic difficulties.

This was just the time when a new wave of ideas was sweeping the Western world, and in particular, the young. We were excited by New Left ideas of decentralised socialism, angered by the discovery of the environmental problems industrial societies were causing, and began taking a new look at the relationships between men and women.

> **You** Yes, I think I get the picture. You're an ageing hippie. But isn't all this a little self-indulgent? I wasn't expecting an autobiography.
>
> **Me** Please be patient. I'm getting quite near the time when the main ideas in this book began to emerge, but I think this background is necessary for you to understand how they came about.

In early 1971 I moved to England, with my wife and daughter. I was a Lecturer in Electronics, Design and Communication at the Open University (OU), just formed as the first distance-learning university and aimed at adults who had missed their chance to go to university and were learning at home.

Many of us young academic staff were determined to bring our new environmental insights into teaching. We felt that part of our mission was to produce a much more integrated form of education to our students, especially as we saw that advanced technology was intimately involved in the environmental destruction that disturbed us. Our first-year course had a strong environmental flavour to it, quite unlike conventional engineering courses of that time.

During the mid-1970s a group of us decided to produce our 'grand course', which we referred to as the Human Ecology Course. We wanted to put environmental issues into their context: show their historical and social roots. We were clear that it wasn't just ignorance that was the problem. We saw a great contradiction between what was considered desirable for the economy and desirable for the environment and social wellbeing.

You Isn't that still the case?

Me Absolutely. That remains the big issue and will be central.

Our team set about researching and developing the background material from many disciplines. There was no obvious niche for a non-linear circuit theorist, so I began to look into processes of social change and into the roots of economic behaviour. I read extensively in the anthropological literature and was fascinated by the variety of human cultures. Many were warlike, but many were extremely peaceful and gentle with crime unknown.

Clearly, the aggressive, competitive nature of human nature as it now appears in western cultures was neither inevitable nor the full extent of human possibilities. The forms of economic behaviour were very varied too, with systems of formalised gift-giving very prevalent, and many systems of symbolic exchange with money-like features. Clearly, the idea that money came about as a great advance over primitive barter totally misunderstood the nature of early cultures and the forces that held them together. All of this will come up later.

For many reasons, personal and otherwise, the human ecology course was never produced. I've always thought of it as unfinished business, which this book is an attempt to continue. The course leader, Mike Hussey (to whom this book is dedicated), took extended study leave, with the intention of writing a book that would form the basis of the course at a later date. He collected material on economics, development, psychology and many other areas. One day in the spring of 1976, he had what he experienced as a tremendous breakthrough. Suddenly, in a momentary flash of insight, all the pieces fitted together.

You Are you saying he had a mystical experience?

Me Perhaps in an earlier age it would have been seen that way. I'd rather leave it as I've described it.

12

Any previous ideas about blaming groups or organisations as the cause of environmental or other social problems fell away. Instead, he could see people caught in chains, or perhaps webs of circumstances, each of which led to other circumstances, endlessly recreating the same patterns. A key element in this was the way in which people's ideas and relationships were formed and shaped by the words and concepts they used. Communication and conversation were at the root of the problem.

The flash of insight was far more than an understanding of what was going wrong, for implicit in that was the possibility that it could be put right. Getting the communication right seemed to hold the possibility of getting relationships right at all levels. Mike immediately began talking about a 'semantic unity network' where people had a shared understanding of critical issues between them.

> **You** Hold on! You are going much too fast. I have a general sense of what you are saying, but it certainly isn't clear.
>
> **Me** Sorry, I'm anticipating some of the key ideas of the book here. It should get clearer.

During that period I spent a lot of time helping Mike develop his ideas. For many years I expected Mike Hussey to write his own book, but that never happened. Then he died suddenly in 1990, leaving a mass of notes but no book.

During the 1980s and 90s, my career took on a new direction. I had become one of the OU's pioneers in the use of computer communications for distance learning, specialising in collaborative learning on-line. I saw this as an opportunity to try out some of our insights into the communications process. I foresaw the possibility of on-line communities linking like-minded but isolated people, like our distance learning students.

This book brings together those two parts of my career: the interest in social and environmental change and the use of computers to support collaborative communities.

This book also builds upon recent parts of my life that are personal rather than professional. In the early 1990s I started going to various festivals and camps for music and dance, mostly in the south-west of England. I met a new partner at one of these. She was in the process of setting up a similar music and dance camp in eastern England. We worked on these together for several years.

About 500 people would attend these events. We camped in groups of between 20 and 40 people in a circle around a common campfire for about 10 days. We cooked communally and socialised around that fire. We lived much closer to the elements than we were used to. The social setting, with its tribe-like camp divided into band-like camping circles, was much closer to that of our pre-historic ancestors than we were used to.

Among the various special qualities of these camps was that they encouraged a sense of instant community. A culture of self-organising mutual support grew up among the campers. A mixture of music, dance and creative play pervaded the practical work of preparing the food, keeping the place clean, caring for the children – and even cleaning the toilets. Some of the people who came to these events felt it changed their lives. Many felt they wanted to extend the kind of community there more widely into their lives. I thought of those camps as the nursery schools of the new culture I was dreaming about, and which this book explores.

Preface to the Second Edition

In the 12 years since I wrote the first edition much has changed in the world, in ways that make the ideas and visions in this book appear more urgent, acceptable and possible. That is why I am writing this second edition.

We are hitting the limits of the Earth in ways that people can see, with the melting of the Arctic, extreme weather events becoming common, huge pressure on food supplies, and more (see Chapter 4). The money system and the economy are on the edge of meltdown, with a collapse possible at any time. Public trust in the banks and the money system are so low that the radical ideas about money in this book might seem more acceptable.

Nonetheless, the mainstream ideas of a competitive economy, with economic growth as its goal are still totally dominant, and unquestioned by politicians, business leaders and mainstream media. Worse still, there has been a defensive reaction against any questioning of these ideas that has even pushed climate change off the agenda, as for example, in the 2012 US presidential election. At least, there are some faint hints that this may be changing.

At the same time, people have become far more closely linked electronically, through social networks and mobile phones. Many of the ingredients of a collaborative culture are here, just waiting to be put together.

As to my own more recent activities. I have now retired from the Open University and have been working on various community projects: food projects and others in the town I live in, and wider projects. In particular, I have been active in the Transition Network. In 2005, Rob Hopkins and a group of like-minded people in South West England started 'Transition Town Totnes' a 'community response to peak oil and climate change'. (See more on this in Chapter 14.) From small beginnings, it has grown to a world-wide movement, clearly catching an important mood in people looking for progressive change. I served a four-year term on the Board of Trustees of the Transition Network, which provides support for this movement. If the camps were the nursery schools of the new culture, the Transition Movement, along with very many similar groups and projects around the world, are its primary schools where we learn practical starting points.

But while I am clear that these projects are starting points, I have also learned how difficult it is for them to grow and thrive in a context where the mainstream economy still dominates. (For example, my food projects struggle to compete with the supermarkets.) So I have come to the reluctant conclusion that these starting points are unlikely to become significant until the economic collapse that I see as imminent actually occurs. Then the real significance of these starting points, and the visions in this book, also becomes clearer. The stronger they are, the easier it will be for the world to escape the worst effects of a collapse, to come to a soft landing in the kind of society we all dream about.

2 Introduction to eGaia

The problems which humanity has created for the natural world and for itself are extremely severe. They are bad enough that the metaphor of a global cancer seems appropriate. Although our environmental problems have been in the public consciousness since the 1960s, it is only now that their full severity is becoming appreciated.

Many people are writing and working to counteract this global cancer. This book introduces the image of eGaia. It is an unashamedly Utopian image, of humanity living in harmony with the planet and in harmony with itself – a genuinely peaceful, sustainable world based around co-operation and community through enhanced communication rather than conflict, competition and war.

Massive problems require radical solutions. Tinkering around the edges won't have much effect. The radical Utopian image of eGaia both clarifies the present problems and provides a pointer to practical steps in that direction: co-operative social groupings, information systems, improving human skills of communication and relationships.

The image of eGaia is of the Earth coming to function with the coherence and wholeness of an organism with humanity analogous to its nervous system. The parts of an organism don't fight each other or destroy the health of the whole. A nervous system is as much controlled by its body as it controls the body. It is part of the body and responds to its needs.

The 'e' in eGaia is there because a nervous system is a communication system. If humans are the nerve cells of a global nervous system, then our electronic communication technologies will enable us to connect to each other in a way rich enough to form locally and globally self-organising and self-regulating social structures.

To convey a first sense of the overall message of this book first demands two metaphors – global cancer and global nervous system – but most of the book will be much more concrete.

You Yes, they are quite emotional metaphors, and they don't fit together. How can a cancer turn into a nervous system?

Me I'll try to give a first answer to your question by mixing my metaphors even more. Do you know how a caterpillar changes into a butterfly?

A caterpillar is completely unlike a butterfly. It is a soft, fat creature, with a body of many segments and a pair of legs on each, which crawls slowly along plants spending its life eating. A butterfly has a small, hard three-segmented body with a pair of legs on each segment and wonderful colourful wings. It flies about pollinating flowers and looking for a mate.

Me You could say the caterpillar lives for food and the butterfly lives for love!

How could such a radical transformation happen? When conditions are right, the caterpillar creates a cocoon around itself and starts its metamorphosis. Triggered by hormonal signals, small areas of its body called 'imaginal disks' begin to grow into the various parts of the butterfly. Simultaneously, the rest of the caterpillar begins to dissolve into its component chemicals, providing the raw materials for the growing butterfly. All this is carefully co-ordinated so that the growing parts link up to form a coherent organism.

The analogy with the Earth is only loose. Unfortunately, there is no protective cocoon. The dissolving of the caterpillar body is analogous to many of the breakdowns caused by the global cancer. It is well underway and is probably irreversible. The imaginal disks are the huge number of organisations and initiatives working to create a sustainable world and a peaceful world. Their influence is only marginal now, but their growth is stimulated by the breakdowns. This book is about how to inspire their growth and help them link up through the development of a communications-based global nervous system.

The metaphor also implies that the results of the transformation will be something completely new, neither a return to some mythical ancient golden age nor business-as-usual but with more environmental awareness. There is no doubt that most of humanity desires a transition to a genuinely peaceful, sustainable Earth. Of course, many caterpillars don't make it through to the butterfly stage, and there is no guarantee that we will succeed in transforming the Earth. But what else is there to do which is as important or exciting?

OUTLINE OF THE BOOK

This second edition of eGaia is being published as an eBook in four parts, similar to the four parts of the first edition. This first part lays out the main ideas which are then filled out by parts 2 – 4.

Part 1 From global cancer to global nervous system

Chapters 1 and *2* are the *Preface* and this *Introduction*.

Chapter 3 A taste of an eGaian future jumps right in with a preview of how it all might work in an imaginary community of the future – 'Pinecone Partnership'. The story takes the best ideas from many current projects and reports and takes them to the next level. Could this be a prototype for a social breakthrough?

Chapter 4 Humanity as a global cancer uses a series of quotations from experts in various areas to give the bad news:

• how we are destroying the natural world

• the ways in which humanity is at war with itself

Chapter 5 It's the economy, stupid! separates the 'real economy' from the money system. It contrasts the present with the vision in the fictional story to show how our money-driven, globalised economy perpetuates the global cancer.

Chapter 6 eGaian principles picks up on the main issues in the preceding chapters and turns them into organising principles for an eGaian world.

Part 2 Context: The five-billion-year story

Chapter 7 Symbiosis and competition is a brief history of the Earth and the evolution of life on it. Its function is to counter the crude view of evolution as shaped only by competition, 'nature red in tooth and claw'. It shows the dual role of competition and symbiosis in the evolution of life.

The Big Bang plus evolution is our modern, scientific creation myth. It is a real shame that the popular version of it has conflict and random change as the central image. This re-write puts symbiosis, collaboration and the growth of order at its centre, so that it provides a sense of direction and hope for the future.

Chapter 8 The co-operative ape favours a positive view of human evolution – collaboration rather than competition. It counteracts the view that the ideas in this book aren't possible because 'the world isn't like that... people aren't like that... conflict and competition are inherent in the way nature works and the way people work'.

You Yes, I bet people think you are completely naïve!

Me Sometimes they do. And if you look at the world today and read about past civilisations it doesn't surprise me. But I think that there is more to the whole picture than most people realise, as I will try to show. There is a difference between the ways things are now and have been recently, and the way they are inherently and necessarily.

Chapter 9 Towards the global cancer traces the stages in the transition from the co-operative ape to global cancer.

Part 3 An eGaian guide: philosophy and principles

Chapter 10 eGaian relationships starts from philosophical first principles to show how convergent communication and mutual understanding enable people to form more coherent views of the world, and thus function effectively. It sets a foundation for a collaborative social structure.

Chapter 11 A peaceful Earth compares cultures in which conflicts are rare and easily handled (because conflict resolution is built into the culture), with those in which conflict is endemic. It describes basic principles of conflict resolution based upon the experience of practitioners.

Chapter 12 A sustainable Earth is a largely practical review of ways in which the sustainability of the Earth might be improved if humanity made that a real priority, building upon much research over recent decades. It pays special attention to food production, sustainable methods of producing goods and energy use.

Chapter 13 A co-operative economy describes organising principles for co-operative economic structures that create a stable, self-correcting economy. It will show ways to use information systems to replace much of the function of money: to provide better measures of cost, of people's social contributions and the other ingredients needed to organise an economy.

> **You** An economy without money? I will read that chapter carefully. This seems to me to be most far-fetched point you are making. I will need a lot of convincing.

> **Me** I do believe an economy without money is possible and desirable, but I am not actually going that far. I think we need to tame our money system with information (think of online ratings and reviews, for example), and remove the worst aspects with new forms of money. The key aspect is that it is co-operative, not competitive.

Part 4 Making eGaia happen

Chapter 14 Starting points is about current 'imaginal disks' – what is happening now that is consistent with the ideas in the eGaian guide: the beginnings of a global communication system, of a global sense of identity and of a sense of symbiosis or mutual support between human cultures. It concludes with a case study, of the Transition Network, that is growing rapidly around the world and embodies many of the eGaian principles.

Chapter 15 The next big steps gives a speculative view of what could take the starting points on to a new level. It is about linking them in mutual support through a community exchange system. This could be the crucial next step that takes the starting points in the previous chapter, links them up so they have critical mass and can take off to become mainstream.

Chapter 16 Summary: Towards an eGaian Earth gives a brief summary of the book and some concluding remarks.

> **You** You really expect the major corporations and democratic governments, much less repressive ones, to voluntarily join your co-operative world?

> **Me** I think some might, and some are beginning to do so as the full weight of the disaster that we are in becomes so obvious it

can't be brushed away. But the mental traps, the beliefs in the desirability and even necessity of our competitive market economy are extremely strong. As I write this second edition, I find I have become more cynical. The positive change so many of us desire might only come about on the wave of collapse of much of our current financial system. I think we are already pushing the natural world into instability in many ways, and this, combined with the instability in our global economy, is likely to trigger a financial crash. While that will be truly awful, it may be the only way we can get out of the mental traps that keep us from creating the kind of world we really want.

Or maybe not. I don't believe the future is knowable. The global cancer that is our present human culture may make the planet a miserable place to live for most of humanity or may even lead to the extinction of humans among the many other life forms that are being lost. Those who understand the possibilities at least have the choice to work for an eGaian future.

3 A taste of an eGaian future

What might it be like at some time in the future, when much of the change to an eGaia society had occurred? What might life be like with humanity functioning as a global nervous system? As this is still an imagined answer to the 'miracle question', we must resort to fiction.

Yes So now you are a Utopian novelist.

Me Not even a short story writer I'm afraid, so apologies if my characters are two-dimensional. The story is there to bring alive the social principles. It will introduce ideas that will be developed more fully later in the book. It will serve as a contrast in *Chapter 5 It's the economy stupid*, to clarify some of the madnesses in the current economic system. It inevitably embodies my fantasies and tastes and a lot of detail is very arbitrary and is just for fun. As you read it, you may find that you like the social principles, but would prefer a different tale.

The point of the story is to show some possible mechanisms:

- *peace* – how can a community handle the conflicts and problems which arise between people while maintaining a sense of mutual concern and understanding?

- *sustainability* – how could a community organise itself in such a way as to take into account the needs of the natural world – but without leading an extremely basic, ascetic life?

- *the right goals* – how could a community use communications to organise itself economically in a way which is directly determined by the needs of the natural world and humanity, rather than indirectly through monetary exchange? Can co-operative structures provide the choice and efficiency supposedly offered by competitive markets?

This tale is set some time in the future, in a world which has moved a long way towards an eGaian society, for reasons that will be explained. It is a tale of a day in the life of some of the members of 'Pinecone Partnership', a group of perhaps several hundred people in a small provincial town in some western country. It is one of many such networks in the town, all loosely linked to each other locally and to larger global networks of different kinds.

MARI

Mari is a young girl, recently turned 16, who is just joining Pinecone Partnership in her own right. She has been using it through her parents' accounts since she was small, so she knows a lot of its members already. She has just completed an introductory training and is about to attend a joining ceremony.

Mari is very excited because she has just received a new phone, the first she has owned personally. She muses that in her mother's youth, young people had their own phones from a younger age, but now life is more austere in material goods. She sees that it is a vintage wePhone 25, one of the earliest with fully recyclable and upgradable parts. She opens the case and finds that she is the third owner, and that it still has a few of its original chips. She begins to think how she could customise it.

She switches it on, holds it up to her face so it can see her eyes and makes her 'ID face'. It quickly flashes up her personal icon. It has recognised her! She puts it in its cradle, where it rapidly downloads all her usual files and apps.

It is time for her joining ceremony. She connects to it on the phone, and quickly flips through the other young people who are part of it. Several are her good friends.

The ceremony is run by Keith, one of the elders of the Partnership, whom she has seen several times when he visited her school. She listens carefully:

"I am delighted to welcome all of you young people, most of whom I have met, to full membership of Pinecone Partnership. You are part of the first generation to have grown up in our new collaborative world society. You have the tools and the education to make it a success, and we are relying on you.

You were all born after the traumatic years of the late twenty-teens, when the old competitive economy and top-down governments collapsed. You have heard this before, but I'll review it for this ceremony.

The more thoughtful people of my generation had been watching in horror as the world ignored the dangers to the environment, until extreme weather began to make some places uninhabitable and to badly disrupt global food supplies, while supplies of fuel became more and more expensive. There were wars and ethnic conflicts, and the growing numbers in extreme poverty lead to lots of unrest. The world money system, which was hugely unstable anyway, lurched from crisis to crisis until it finally collapsed, and took with it the real economy – many of the businesses and services we all relied upon.

In desperation, people joined together in their local communities, pooling their resources to help one other. Many new community groups formed, for food, sharing goods, transport, child care, and all sorts of mutual help. People rediscovered the importance of working together in their communities. New forms of community exchange and local money sprang up. Fortunately, there were many starting points for them to learn from, and enough of the social networks and communications survived so that the best ideas spread rapidly around the world.

The apps we now use all the time – that make exchange in our communities so easy – were developed and everyone started using them. That is really what saved us.

It was like a huge mental cloud lifting from humanity: People could finally see that the old ideas of chasing money, of everyone competing with everyone else, and of power politics, were a madness that had dominated humankind for millennia.

The problems of those days are far from over. There is massive reconstruction to do. Many people are still struggling. In a perverse way, we are lucky that the economy collapsed when it did. Had it happened 10 years later, the damage to the environment might have been irreversible. It is so sad that it took a collapse to create the change, rather than a managed transition, which would have saved many lives and much destruction.

Now, at least we have a chance to repair the damage, and to build the kind of society people have dreamed about for thousands of years. It is up to us all!"

Mari finds that she has several new apps in her phone. She now has her own account in Pinecone Partnership, where she will get most of her daily needs met: food, clothes, transport and all the stuff that is made locally. She won't have to pay for any of that in money, but she will use her phone to record what she receives and gives to the community. She will be expected to contribute a reasonable number of hours of work each week, keeping the giving and receiving roughly in balance, and to keep up a good public reputation. She thinks about the kinds of work she may do, perhaps on Elderberry Farm, or Watermelon House looking after the old people. She looks at the other members, and sees that many of her school friends and friends of her parents are there.

And she now has a new account in the regional bank run by the Walnut River Valley Network, that covers a large bio-region in her part of the country. She sees that she already has a few partners, some young people she has met on trips, and some she knows through her parents and their friends. It has its own currency, the Walnut, which she will be able to earn and spend. Most of what she wants that isn't produced in Pinecone Partnership will come through that. Again, she will have to be careful about her reputation, but she will always be dealing with people she trusts, and whom she knows or are friends of people she knows.

And there is her Eco account! This is the new global currency that links people all over the world, managed by the new World Eco Bank. She thinks about the special treats she can get from that, and perhaps the trips she might take, and wonders how she can earn some Ecos. She finds she has a few partners there already, from those exchange students that stayed with her family a few years ago, and a few that her parents have arranged for her.

And finally there is her Footprint account ('environmental footprint' is based on the impact on the environment of an object or activity). She looks at it and finds that her parents have transferred all her favourite clothes and things from their accounts to hers. As she looks through each item she can see that it includes two ratings, one for its impact on the Earth, and one for the number of hours of human effort it took to create. Her footprint is the total of the footprints of all the things in her account.

Mari has grown up with the idea that a sensible person tries to satisfy their needs while keeping their footprint at a reasonable level for their age.

> **You** Let's see if I've got the points here. You have an economy where people mostly deal with others to whom they are connected as partners, in several groups, one very local, one regional and then global. The most local doesn't seem to use money, but the other two have their own currencies, including a global currency. They seem to use their phones rather than cash for everything. People also have records of the 'Footprint', which seems to measure their social and environmental impact.

> **Me** Yes, that's about right. There are different kinds of trading relationship, some more like a 'gift economy', others more like money, but always based on personal relationship and with a strong element of reputation, so that where money is used it doesn't dominate. And 'Footprint' measures real cost: effect on the Earth and on other people, expressed directly, rather than (as now) hidden or ignored within monetary cost. And apps on the social networks are the key to making it work.

ALBERT

Albert is 49 and manages Apple Transport, a small firm he built up that was once a car showroom and garage. He nearly lost the business during the big crash, but because he had such a good reputation, he was supported first by the community and then by the new regional bank. For all practical purposes the business is a co-operative 'owned' by the community it serves, including both its customers and its employees, who are intensely loyal to it.

Apple Transport takes full responsibility for all aspects of its customers' vehicles. It gets them, services and updates them and disposes of them.

Albert spends about three days each week working for Apple Transport, which is considered to be a lot. A couple of his employees share his managerial responsibilities and stand in for him when needed. Albert often spends another day or two working at other small jobs which interest him. He also helps out at the market garden/farm and at the town hospital.

He starts each day on his tablet, looking at Apple Transport's sign-up sheets on Pinecone Partnership. First he checks that enough people have signed up to work for him over the next few days. He has a workforce of about 5-10 each week, most of whom work a few days each week. They are drawn from a much larger pool who work for him from time to time. He always has enough in reserve to cover absences or peak workloads. The workforce is variable but well organised and reliable. Many of them work at more than one transport vehicle co-operative locally. All of his employees put in some hours as part of their contribution to Pinecone Partnership, but they also get paid flexibly in Walnuts and Ecos, as they need them.

He has to pay in Walnuts for standard parts that are made regionally, and in Ecos for electronic parts that are made in large international factories. He earns Walnuts and Ecos by doing work for people outside Pinecone Partnership.

Most vehicles are electric these days, which are much more efficient than older petrol vehicles. While their batteries are being charged they act as storage to balance the variability of the wind and wave-generated electricity that power them. A few use bio-fuels. Most vehicles are shared or are owned by businesses or by public transport. Many people use bicycles and walk when they can, while those who are less able use electric bicycles or public transport.

There is a rating system on-line which most of the customers use after every visit. Albert prides himself that his garage and his employees almost always receive very high ratings. That is the basis of his very strong customer loyalty. He and his staff carefully check out each case of a low rating to see what they can learn from it. Can they improve their working

27

practices? Does someone need more training? Was it a misunderstanding and if so, how can they avoid that in future?

Albert sees that he could do with two more workers for Friday because a lot of customers have booked in. He sends a text message to all his regulars pointing this out. If this doesn't do the trick within the next day or so, he will make a few phone calls and sort it out. And then next Monday almost no-one has booked in. So he emails two of the staff due to work then and tells them not to come in. He hopes they will be happy to have the day off.

He looks through the messages in the Regional Transport Network, which links all the firms like his as well as the researchers in the university and other related trade networks. They all support each other as much as they can, as they aren't in competition. Each has its own niche: its regular customers, its own specialities.

There are regular meetings of people from each firm, where they review any problems they are having, advise each other on solutions, and work out how they can support each other, such as buying specialised equipment that they can share between them. If there are any disputes between members, the Regional Transport Network has people who can help solve them constructively.

As a senior person in his industry locally, Albert has also qualified as an inspector, and he signs up to inspect two firms in the area. He also puts Apple Transport down for inspection. With the inspections, customer ratings, and research information he gets, his firm is kept on its toes and is far more up-to-date and efficient than it ever was in the old days of competition. There is no central regulation needed, and through the regional and global links it has the strengths of multi-nationals of earlier generations.

He has a group of customers who enjoy having older vehicles, and with his help, can usually keep them going indefinitely. All his vehicles use fuel very efficiently, and with all the recycling of parts and the sharing of vehicles, they add very little to each customer's footprint.

It is quite a light day for Apple Transport. There are only two mechanics around, so Albert helps them out. He has farmed out a couple of jobs to another firm that had a few cancellations.

> **You** Clearly transport is much more environmentally friendly here. But the main thing that strikes me is flexibility. People seem to work when it suits them.

> **Me** Yes, it's important that people are motivated to work because they like the work and because of the respect it gives them. The workload can be adjusted either up or down to follow demand. Albert has neither need nor desire to advertise or to try to influence demand. The business is driven by quality and service, not making money. Quality is maintained by feedback and peer inspection, not fear of loss of customers or government regulation. That makes it function as an error-correcting control system so it is stable and resilient. Socially, it has some of the qualities of an extended family.

EAVIS

Eavis is the manager of Elderberry Farm. Now 60, he has been a farmer all of his life and comes from a farming family. He often reflects on the complete transformation of farming within his lifetime. During the crash, he, like many other farmers, very nearly lost his land. Farms are mostly now owned by community land trusts, with the farmers as stewards, managing them for the benefit of the community. He was very unhappy about that for a long time, but has come to see that it actually works a lot better for him. He is a real farmer now, not a businessman.

The word farm doesn't really do it justice anymore. In a way it is a modern high-tech version of what medieval estates used to provide. Elderberry Farm is one of the principal sources of food (vegetables, grains, meat) for Pinecone Partnership and other local networks. But it does much more. Its woodlands provide fuel for the community and wood for furniture and building materials. The wood is also used as the raw material for the chemicals which Pinecone Plastics needs, replacing the oil an earlier generation would have used. The farm is a re-cycling centre for organic wastes which are converted to fertilisers and 'biochar' to absorb carbon and which also produce gas and alcohol as fuels. Up on Pinecone Ridge is a row of large wind turbines producing electricity. Elderberry Farm is a major supplier of fuel and electricity to homes, factories and workshops in the area. The result of all this is that Elderberry Farm helps the people of Pinecone Partnership keep their ecological footprint very low.

The farming methods have changed radically too. There has been extensive planting of trees and perennial plants, as part of the world's desperate attempt to remove some of the carbon dioxide from the atmosphere that it put there before the crash. It still isn't clear whether global warming can be stopped.

Woodlands have been extended to include fruit, nuts, berries and many other perennial edible plants. They are the home to deer, pigs, and various other animals that live wild and are culled for food by the farm. Organic agro-forestry has become the norm, with even the remaining fields looking more like mixed grassland than earlier single crop farming.

The farm now requires a lot more labour than it did in the 20th century. However, this has not proved to be a problem, as Eavis supplements his small core of skilled staff with large numbers of casual workers.

The farm has been planted with an eye to aesthetics as well as food efficiency. It is now considered very beautiful and is a popular place for Pinecone people, who come to work there, just hang out, or participate in various events.

Eavis used to enjoy pop festivals and camps in his youth. He has turned Elderberry Farm into a place where people come to work during the day and to be entertained and party in the evenings. He regularly books entertainment and theatre workshops, catering for different interests on different dates. In between, people come and entertain themselves. Elderberry Farm has become as popular with performers as with its farm labourers. They often wander amongst the labourers, with songs and street theatre.

He gets on his computer to check on the bookings for the next week. He sees that Bertha and her friends have booked again. They are regulars and so have experience with the work. They don't need to be paid, as their work is part of their contribution to Pinecone Partnership. He looks at the list of tasks coming up and selects a few he thinks would appeal to Bertha's gang. There is a tremendous variety due to the rich nature of the farm. His skill, as a good modern farm manager, is to keep the farm as near as he can to a natural ecosystem while intervening just enough to make most of its produce of value to people.

> **You** This farm is an environmentalist's dream. It's organic, feeds local people, looks good, supplies energy, reduces carbon dioxide. I'm not sure quite what is the point of turning it into a festival, though.

> **Me** The point of the festival atmosphere is to create motivation to work. Farm labour is made attractive by spreading it widely among the people the farm feeds and making the work fun. Isn't that better than forcing it upon the poor? It's a different kind of relationship than you usually get between a farm, its customers and workers. That way the issue of competition with other farms nearby or across the world doesn't arise.

HENRIETTA

Henrietta is 76 and lives in Watermelon House, a large co-operative hostel owned by Pinecone Partnership. It caters largely for single people and couples without children, but also includes a few families. It was converted into a hostel from a redundant hospital. It has sections that are adapted to the needs of the elderly and those with disabilities.

Henrietta is partially disabled physically, as a result of a stroke a few years ago, but her mind is sharp. She likes making an active contribution to the community. Pinecone Partnership has opened opportunities for this in ways that would have been impossible for older and disabled people in earlier times. She likes living in a mixed community with people of all ages. She often works in the kitchen in Watermelon House, as she has always loved cooking. Often when there is cooked food left over, she puts it in small containers, freezes it and sends it to the Sustainable Supermarket. She has almost no need for money, as Pinecone Partnership supplies all her regular needs.

Henrietta spends much of her time organising the Transport Users Co-op. It functions as a self-organising taxi and delivery service for Pinecone Partnership, as very few people now have their own vehicles. The co-op owns a small fleet of cars, mini-buses and vans, mostly electric, which are supplied and cared for by Apple Transport.

It is heavily used by children and people with limited mobility, saving huge effort for parents and carers. They like and trust it because they generally know the drivers. Henrietta and the drivers take their user ratings very seriously and try to learn from any low ones.

Today she will be getting a visit from Francoise's young son, whom she often sees. He helps her clean her room, and enjoys the stories she tells him about the bad old days before Pinecone Partnership. She was a real consumer and always had the latest gadget. Now she misses them, but the social benefits far outweigh that.

She tells him about her own mother, and how difficult things were when she was old and infirm. In those days, old people had to rely on help from the government, from strangers paid out of taxation. Now the community looked after its own, as it did in earlier generations.

> **You** Interesting... this is a clear mixture of the environmental and the social. You've got a responsive, friendly, semi-public transport system which must save a lot of fuel. If it worked well, some people wouldn't want their own cars.
>
> **Me** Yes, there is concern for the Earth and a co-operative social structure. And the way the Transport Co-op is organised illustrates the error-correcting feedback system working to the right goals.

FRANCOISE

Francoise is 38 and lives with her partner, Gerry and their two children. Their older son, who is 12, often spends afternoons at Watermelon House, where he has several adopted 'grandparents' among the elderly residents, including Henrietta. He runs errands and does odd jobs for them. They help look after him, teach him and feed him.

Both children have busy social lives. Francoise frequently uses the apps on her phone to arrange for them to be taken and collected by the Transport Users Co-op organised by Henrietta. But more often they walk or cycle. These days traffic is so much lighter and there is so much less street crime that Francoise thinks that is quite safe.

Francoise usually works for several days each week in the Pinecone Plastics factory. It is still legally a part of an old-style multi-national that was re-organised during the period of the crash. It has close links with their other factories and research labs around the world so keeps the benefits of global scale. At the same time, it has become a co-operative, integrated within Pinecone Partnership. After struggling for years, it has recently been upgraded with the most modern automated equipment and serves a wide range of needs for Pinecone people.

Organising the upgrade was a major job for Francoise a year ago, but she had a lot of help. She had to find out the best equipment to get, and make arrangements with their suppliers, who mostly gave her credit in the regional and global currencies, which she then needed to earn. She had to arrange some guarantees from the regional bank. She remembers that this was a lot more complicated than smaller changes, where she could draw upon members and businesses within the Partnership for labour and materials without needing to pay them or raise funds.

The factory is a large modern building which, like many others, is roofed with solar panels. Some panels are photovoltaic and produce electricity; others are thermal to heat water. It also has an algae plant that produces liquid fuels and removes carbon dioxide from the atmosphere, as everyone is desperate to do that now. Most of its additional needs for fuel and electricity are supplied by Elderberry Farm.

It tends to adjust its workload seasonally, increasing its output when the wind or the solar energy are greater, and reducing output when they are lower.

Most of the raw materials needed by Pinecone Plastics come from recycled plastic from components it has made in the past. Most of its output is designed for this. Additional raw materials are made by chemically digesting wood and other vegetable matter from Elderberry Farm, and are part of the money-free partnership. Some comes from farther afield, and are paid for in Walnuts or Ecos. All of this helps keep the ecological footprint of its products very low. One of Francoise's regular tasks is to find sources for specialised materials from collaborating factories and farms in the region.

Today she is working on some new car body panels that Albert's Apple Transport has ordered. She doesn't have the design for that model in her library, so sends a message to the other plastics factories in the region asking for help. In her inbox there is a short article from the regional research labs describing an easier way to clean out used moulds. That will save her and all the other plastics factories hours. In the old days, one firm would use information like that to gain competitive advantage over the others.

She finds a request for dustbins from a factory in the next county, (its machine has broken down) and offers to produce them.

>**You** Another environmentalist's dream! It uses renewable energy and local raw materials.

>**Me** Yes, and re-use and recycling means it provides its customers with a good material living standard at low environmental cost. Also, notice that it responds to the requests from its customers and that there is mutual support between similar businesses. By co-operating, not competing, they can be much more efficient. They don't need to go out looking for customers. Its workload varies with the seasons, with the weather, with demand. The communication networks are what make it practical. All this makes it very much more efficient than today's businesses in serving the community and the environment, but not in making money.

GERRY

Gerry is one of those energetic people who can't stop doing things. He spends several days working in the Sustainable Supermarket, but then invariably signs up for several shifts around the community. He often drives the minibuses and vans for Henrietta's Travel Co-op, he and his rugby mates take shifts together working on the roads and parks (always a good laugh), and he occasionally shows off his newly developed cooking skills in the hospital kitchen.

To help at mealtimes, Gerry often brings back frozen meals from the Sustainable Supermarket. These are not the old-fashioned, highly processed kind but are usually locally made by enthusiastic cooks in Pinecone Partnership.

The Sustainable Supermarket work provides him with his major challenges. It is very different from the supermarkets of old. Although it is still legally part of one of the big three from the early 21st century, in practice it is more like a medieval marketplace, serving its local community. It is a distribution place for most of what is produced by Pinecone Plastics, Elderberry Farm and other local organisations: food, clothing, goods, everything. Most are locally produced and where they serve members of Pinecone Partnership, don't involve money. A significant proportion may come from anywhere in the world, usually paid in Ecos. It has strong links with distributors and other sustainable supermarkets.

Parts of the supermarket and its garden are full of small stalls from local workshops and other enterprises. This includes furniture, craft items, refurbished and re-designed clothing, renewed appliances. Anything that can be repaired, recycled or improved passes through it. It is a main collection place for re-cycling. This began to grow during the crash, when people couldn't really buy much new.

The food is mostly fresh, organic and local, but there are plenty of cooked meals, made by those Pinecone people who love cooking. The result is that it helps the people of Pinecone Partnership live well while keeping their ecological footprint low.

As markets have always been, it is an important meeting place. It has been beautifully decorated, with sculptures and other artwork. There is always entertainment of some sort, and lots of stalls.

The challenge for Gerry is to provide the best match he can of supply and demand. Through the social networks he keeps careful track of what people want and what is available. He often puts out polls and questionnaires asking about what people want in the future. People routinely rate what they have received so he has feedback on quality and satisfaction.

The bulk of what the sustainable supermarket provides is routine and in plentiful supply. That includes the basic food staples, household goods and appliances. Much of this is ordered through people's phones. They either collect it in person or the supermarket delivers it, helped by the Transport Users Co-op. When people order something the sustainable supermarket doesn't usually carry, Gerry searches through the trade networks to find it. For luxury items, he and the other markets have developed a number of strategies. That batch of a special, new ice cream flavour was offered on a first-come, first-served basis. Jewellery, art and other rare items sometimes circulate, with people holding onto them for a few months, or even just for a special occasion. Sometimes there are prize draws for special items.

> **You** OK, so most things are local. That reduces transport which is good for the environment. But why do you need prize draws? Why don't people simply buy what they want?

> **Me** Gerry tries to match supply and demand as best he can. He doesn't need to influence demand to improve his cash flow. Most of what we use money for is done through information: real costs (footprint), finding out what people want, organising who will do what work, knowing what is available. But some things are scarce and need some form of rationing, such as prize draws. Today they would be 'rationed' to the rich.

CONAN

Conan is 25. He lives with his girlfriend, Delilah, in Watermelon House. Conan and Delilah eat most of their meals in the hostel's large dining room, which caters not only for residents, but also often for their guests or visitors to the community. The dining room walls are an ever-changing art gallery. It is also frequently used for musical and community events. It is a social focus for its residents.

Conan likes doing things with his hands, working with machines and tools. He sees himself as a craftsman and an artist. His work is mostly around the hostel, but he is also a regular worker at Apple Transport. He loves the challenge of taking old cars that no-one wants anymore and updating, repairing and customising them so they will once again be someone's pride and joy.

He starts his day by checking his shifts at Apple Garage, and signs up for the date when his friend Sasha is on. Conan then looks through the list of jobs people have asked for in the hostel. There is that tricky plumbing job with the awkwardly sized pipe. He fills in an order form to have it custom made at Pinecone Plastics factory. A few seconds later a receipt comes back saying it has been booked and will be ready in two days. He then selects two jobs to get on with for the morning, but decides he will spend the afternoon working on his new mural for the dining room.

Conan is troubled by quite dramatic mood swings. Sometimes his temper is easily triggered, and he has a history of violence both to people and to things. People are aware of his difficulties and help him to handle them, partly by helping him avoid situations in which his anger will be triggered. There have been times when his mood has become so dark that he has been put into a secure community for the duration. When he has injured someone, he has been helped to understand fully what he has done, has had to make peace with the victim, and do something agreed to attempt to make up for the injury.

> **You** You have some communal living for those not in families, which makes environmental sense. But the interesting thing is that we now have a villain. Not everyone here is perfect.

> **Me** Conan is not a villain. He is more difficult than most but he lives in a community which has learned to handle him with sympathy and in a way which repairs the emotional and physical damage as best it can. In our world he would

probably have been put into a prison which would have turned him into a bitter but well-trained criminal.

You This strategy must rely upon there being relatively few such people around.

Me Yes it does. They aren't grown and hardened as they are today. Conan didn't grow up with peers who respected and glorified his violence. He always had opportunities to make positive contributions to his community that gave him approval and respect. That is what made his problems manageable. This is an example of society as an error-correcting control system in the social realm. The understanding that is shown to him and that he had to show to his victims is an example of using communication to solve social problems.

DELILAH

Delilah has lived in Watermelon House with Conan for several years. She loves his playfulness and his practical talents. She has had special training to help him handle his darker moods. Like many young people nowadays, she splits her time between various passionate interests. For her, it is dancing. Delilah has had dance training since she was a child. She is very popular in the region, getting bookings for solo performances and as a choreographer running classes and workshops. With the current revival of the arts, the opportunities are much greater than in earlier generations.

Besides dancing, Delilah's main job is as a community banker, working for the Walnut Valley Regional Bank and also as an agent for the World Eco Bank. In practice this means she is a go-between, sorting out agreements between people and businesses that don't know each other. She worked with Francoise, finding people to supply the equipment she needed for the factory upgrade. Her role was to convince them that Francoise was worthy of credit, and that her bank would guarantee the payment if needed.

Money is totally electronic, with payments made largely through people's phones. Accounts become negative when a business or individual needs something big and the debt is paid over an agreed period. Delilah works with clients, helping to work out the most suitable credit limits and payment times. No interest is ever charged for credit, but sometimes there are small fees. Money is never in short supply, as it is created in the process of debts being formed and dissolves as they are repaid.

> **You** So, the money system here is very different. No interest on loans! Money never in short supply!

> **Me** Yes, here the money system serves the community rather than dominating it. It supports exchange where needed.

BERTHA

Bertha is 17 and lives with her family. This morning she looks on the network for confirmation of her booking for the coming weekend at Elderberry Farm. She and her friends go there often to work on the farm while enjoying the music and dance that is laid on for them in the evenings. She loved the last dance workshop she did there with Delilah and knows there will be another one this weekend.

Pinecone Partnership has been a major support for her education, especially in her teenage years. Much of her education has been based around project work, some developed herself. Other projects are devised and set up by her teachers. Many have been collaborative projects, usually including some of her friends, but often with young people in other parts of the country or the world. Through the network she can find other young people to work with her, share information, co-ordinate work, and do background research.

Bertha looks on the network for replies to her application for a trip to an Eastern European country where there are still vestiges of ethnic conflict. This is part of her training in cultural conflict resolution, which she hopes will become one of her main career areas.

From early childhood Bertha (along with all the other children) has been taught the communication skills which people have learned to see as the foundation of social education. Through games and little plays they have learned how to listen, how to put yourself in another's shoes, how to check that you have been understood or understand another. Her current ambitions build on that basic education.

On her trip she will be a trainee in a large team made up of locals and people from around the world. They were assembled in response to reports of the growing popularity of some agitators who were stirring up hatred of an ethnic minority. The team has several main strategies. They look at the discontents among the people who are receptive to the agitators. They acknowledge those discontents and help seek resolution for them. They also use a combination of media events and local community activities to help both groups in conflict to see the others as full people rather than as shadowy hate figures. They create opportunities for both communities to meet and work together socially. The leaders of this team are highly trained and experienced. They know how important it is to get into an area where trouble is brewing early enough, and with enough support and resources from outside. Then they can usually defuse the conflict before the hatred becomes too great on both sides. Bertha hopes she might eventually become that kind of team leader.

Bertha has planned to travel slowly, visiting various places on the way. Through the Accommodation Co-op in Pinecone Partnership she has found the names of people in all the places she plans to visit. They are all friends of people known to Pinecone Partnership who offer temporary room and board to friends of friends, as do many people in Pinecone Partnership. Several have replied offering her rooms. Similarly, she finds messages from the Ride-sharing Co-op offering her lifts for about half of the journeys she will need to make. For the remainder, she books seats for the buses and trains she will be taking and pays for them in Ecos.

> **You** A new tack. You seem to think childhood education about communication is crucial and that really big social problems can be headed off if they are caught early. You must be assuming that the local government and society around the troubled area allow the team in and support it. That wouldn't happen today.

> **Me** This future society is geared up to resolve conflicts, which it accepts as arising regularly. It uses communication to acknowledge people's concerns and promote mutual understanding, rather than imposing solutions by force.

Teaching communications skills is crucial so that people simply don't get caught up in conflicts and difficult relationships as easily as they do today. I cannot over-emphasize this.

JOLINE

Joline is a single woman aged 50 with two grown children. She plays the flute, and frequently is seen wandering the fields and woodlands at Elderberry Farm entertaining the farm workers.

Joline is known throughout the area for her skills as a counsellor and mediator. She works with individuals, couples, families and work groups. She has a reputation as the person to call when conflicts begin to appear in a workplace. With her help, a solution can usually be found before the conflict gets too serious.

She is sometimes called in by the Regional Bank, when there is a dispute over charges and payments. She always works to find a mutually agreed solution. She reflects that this work would have been done by courts in earlier generations. And also, how much simpler transactions are within Pinecone Partnership where there are no money payments.

Another of Joline's interests is helping to co-ordinate the co--operatives and businesses that make up Pinecone Partnership. All of them are autonomous, and make their own decisions about their day-to-day running. But they all affect one another too, and there are sometimes disagreements. Joline calls regular meetings of groups of businesses, like the Plastics factories, and the farms. At these meetings, they review the functioning of all the members, highlighting problems and seeking solutions, planning joint strategies where they could all benefit.

Joline's skill is in helping groups with different views to understand each other's point of view, and then in finding solutions that are acceptable to everyone. The respect in which she is held means people are usually willing to accept her solutions. It sometimes amuses her to think that she is the modern equivalent of a politician. Yet in many ways she is the opposite of old-time politicians, who used to make a point of disagreeing with their rivals.

Most decision-making is the business of the co-ops and other organisations, but issues like land use require the agreement of everyone. There was a proposal to expand the gardens of Watermelon House into what had been a small park. Such decisions are normally made by consensus as much as possible, rather than majority vote, so that majorities cannot impose their will upon minorities.

> **You** This is meant to show how the community is organised co-operatively.
>
> **Me** Yes. Just as our society now has well-understood skills of building roads and repairing them when needed, an eGaian society would need well-understood skills of co-ordinating groups and individuals. This is at least as important as concern for the natural world. It underpins the kind of collaborative society needed to solve our environmental problems.

KEITH

Keith is pushing 60 and for most of his earlier life he was a full-time academic, working at the local university as an environmental scientist.

Now his life is much more varied. He enjoys being able to spend time on more physical pursuits, which keeps him feeling alive and healthy. He often spends time at Elderberry Farm.

Some of Keith's work at Elderberry Farm is physical labouring, for the fun of it and to keep him healthy, but he also works as a scientific adviser. One of Keith's main contributions to Elderberry Farm is to keep in touch through the networks with the scientific community that specialises in agro-forestry farms of that sort. He gets advice when they have problems and learns of new approaches.

Keith is mostly content these days, enjoying his life, but as a scientist, he is also very aware that there are still major environmental problems left. At least, human impact on the Earth is slowing down, with less transport, local production, more recycling, less pollution, renewable energy sources. It's just as well, as with much less oil, farming especially has had to change radically. Much effort has gone into restoring and rebuilding wilderness areas and sea habitats and finding ways to remove carbon dioxide from the atmosphere.

He has seen the major changes in people's attitudes towards consumption. Nowadays, when people consume anything, the effect on their ecological footprint is automatically calculated. It has become a matter of pride to live well while keeping your ecological footprint low.

But far more important for people's everyday lives have been the social changes. The community focus and the communications skills have reduced crime, alienation and have improved family life. Economic uncertainty is rarely a problem and most people do work they enjoy. Perhaps most important of all is the sense of connection to each other and to the Earth. The idea that people function like a nervous system of the Living Earth has taken on an almost religious or spiritual character, adding to the love and joy in all the Earth's peoples.

You Isn't that last bit a little over the top?

Me Sure, this is an over the top story. It's the answer to the miracle question. Do you want to settle for less in your hopes and dreams? This is not a let's-be-miserable-to-save-the-Earth future. I've tried to show how interconnected the environmental and social aspects are, and that solutions to the environmental problems come out of major social changes. Faced with the need for major changes because of the global cancer, surely there is no point in going for some partial solution which still leaves the world full of misery? The answer to the miracle question is the change from humanity as a global cancer to humanity as a global nervous system.

4 Humanity as a global cancer

FORESTS GOING···
SPECIES DYING
OUT·· FRESH
WATER'S DEGRADED
·· GLOBAL WARMING
···EXTENSIVE
POLLUTION·· WARS
··HUNGER···
POVERTY···
CRIME

yeah but
apart from that
things are OK-yeah?

The world is certainly not like the eGaian image today. Nor are the dominant trends in that direction. Humanity is now more like a global cancer than a global nervous system. While climate change is the biggest environmental issue in public consciousness, in fact it is only one of many symptoms of the global cancer. This chapter looks how we are destroying the natural world and also ourselves, to make clear the urgency of change, and the foolishness of trying to preserve those aspects of our present culture that are causing the cancer.

You So this is the gloomy chapter.

Me I'm afraid so. What is worse, for this second edition of eGaia, the cancer is much more advanced. Now the effects of climate change hit many people directly, for example through extreme weather, and the instability in the financial system hits headlines and families all the time.

You will find lots of horrible facts you can use to shock your friends. But at least the chapter ends on a hopeful note, by arguing that the problems are socially created and are thus not inevitable.

A CANCER OF THE NATURAL WORLD

"At some time in the 1970s, humanity as a whole passed the point at which it lived within the global regenerative capacity of the Earth,..." World Wide Fund for Nature [1]

A hundred thousand years or so ago we were one medium-sized mammal among many, with no more effect on the planet than any of the others. We were (and are) one of a handful of species of great ape. Life flourished throughout the seas, the land and the air – forming forests, grasslands, aquatic and other ecosystems.

The planet as a whole has had a limited stability over its five billion year life. Major ecosystems maintained their general form over long periods of time as a result of feedback effects such as predator-prey relationships. This relative stability was punctuated from time to time by periods of very rapid change. There have been five mass extinctions in which most of the species alive at the time were wiped out. The best known extinction was 65 million years ago when the dinosaurs disappeared. There have been major rapid changes of weather and climate such as the start and end of ice ages. These ideas are developed in Part II of this book, *The five billion year story*.

We are now in one of those periods of very rapid change. This time it is due to human activity, which now dominates the world physically and biologically. We are certainly no longer one medium-sized mammal among many.

The concept of 'environmental footprint' has recently been developed to measure the area of land needed to support a person at a given level of technology. On this measure, the wealthier countries already consume on

---

1 *Living Planet Report 2000*, World Wide Fund for Nature, http://www.wwf.org.uk/filelibrary/pdf/livingplanet2002.pdf.

average three times their fair share of sustainable global output.[2] Human population growth and the prospect of development in the poorer countries will make this worse.

Extinction of species

"My greatest fear for our world is that global warming may produce an increased rate of extinction and eventually reach some threshold point, triggering a cascade of mass extinction, a free-fall of death. Each species on the Earth is like a tiny piece in a four-dimensional jigsaw, interlocking with other species," Peter Ward[3]

It is not just the odd pretty butterfly or polar bear that is in danger. The rate at which species are becoming extinct is comparable to that of the great extinctions of the past. The normal background rate of extinctions is about 10 to 25 per year, while now it is probably in the thousands. Expert sources agree:

"The most comprehensive assessment of the world's mammals has confirmed an extinction crisis, with almost 1 in 4 at risk of disappearing forever, according to the recently updated IUCN Red List of Threatened Species. The new study shows at least 1,141 of the 5,487 listed mammals on Earth are known to be threatened with extinction. Overall, the IUCN Red List now includes 44,838 species, of which 16,928 are threatened with extinction (38 %). Of these, 3,246 are in the highest category of threat, Critically Endangered, 4,770 are Endangered and 8,912 are Vulnerable to extinction."[4]

"The World Wide Fund for Nature (WWF) said unless there was co-ordinated action by governments in central Africa and south-east Asia

---

[2] William Rees, "Revisiting Carrying Capacity: Area-Based Indicators of Sustainability", *Population and Environment*, Vol. 17, No. 3, Jan. 1996, Human Sciences Press, Inc.

[3] Peter D Ward, *Rivers in Time, The search for clues to Earth's mass extinctions*, Columbia University Press, New York, 2000, p.82.

[4] Local Action for Biodiversity, http://www.iclei.org/index.php?id=9003

there could be no halt to the dramatic decline in the numbers of great apes – chimpanzees, gorillas, bonobos and orang-utans – and their eventual disappearance."[5]

"Cascade effects occur when the local extinction of one species significantly changes the population sizes of other species, potentially leading to other extirpations."[6]

Loss of natural habitats

Human activities have significantly disturbed the global water, carbon, and nitrogen cycles on which all life depends. Agriculture, industry, and the spread of human settlements have permanently converted extensive areas of natural habitat and contributed to ecosystem degradation through fragmentation, pollution, and increased incidence of pest attacks, fires, and invasion by non-native species.

"Forest cover has been reduced by more than 20 percent worldwide, with some forest ecosystems, such as the dry tropical forests of Central America, virtually gone. More than 50 percent of the original mangrove area in many countries is gone; wet-lands area has shrunk by about half; and grasslands have been reduced by more than 90 percent in some areas. Only tundra, arctic, and deep-sea ecosystems have emerged relatively unscathed."[7]

Damage to agriculture and fisheries

"Agriculture, forestry, and fishing are responsible for 50 percent of all jobs world- wide and 70 percent of the jobs in sub-Saharan Africa, East Asia, and the Pacific. ...Although crop yields are still rising, the underlying condition of agroecosystems is declining in much of the world. Soil degradation is a concern on as much as 65 percent of

[5] *Reuters*, 4 Oct. 1997

[6] World Resources Institute, Washington, D.C.

[7] *A Guide to World Resources 2000-2001, People and Ecosystems, The Fraying Web of Life*, World Resources Institute, Washington, D.C. 2000. http://www.wri.org/publication/world-resources-2000-2001-people-and-ecosystems-fraying-web-life

agricultural land. ...About two-thirds of agricultural land has been degraded in the past 50 years by erosion, salinization, compaction, nutrient depletion, biological degradation, or pollution. About 40 percent of agricultural land has been strongly or very strongly degraded."[8]

"About 80 percent of the world marine fish stocks for which assessment information is available are fully exploited or overexploited. Fish stocks assessed since 1977 have experienced an 11% decline in total biomass globally... . There is also an increasing trend of stock collapses over time, with 14% of assessed stocks collapsed in 2007."[8]

Change to the physical world: climate and weather

The past 15 years or so have seen a remarkable battle on the issue of climate change. On the one hand, the scientific evidence for climate change is completely accepted by virtually all serious scientists who study it, and is increasingly obvious to the general public in the form of the extreme weather events it causes and the melting of the Arctic. On the other hand, there has been a powerful and highly successful campaign of disinformation to discredit the whole idea of climate change, funded principally by the oil industry. The result is that while in the 1990s governments were increasingly taking notice of the dangers of climate change, with the Rio Earth Summit, Agenda 21 and the Kyoto treaty, now they barely pay lip service to it, and it was almost entirely absent from the 2012 US elections.

Here is a small sample of scientific statements:

"The concentration of the main greenhouse gas, carbon dioxide (CO_2), has continued to increase from its pre-industrial concentration of approximately 278 parts per million (ppm) to over 391 ppm in September 2012, *[Author: And more recently hit 400 ppm, that is a 41% increase!]*. The present CO_2 concentration is higher than paleoclimatic

---

[8] *Global Biodiversity Outlook 3 (Convention on Biological Diversity, 2010)* http://www.cbd.int/doc/publications/gbo/gbo3-final-en.pdf

and geologic evidence indicates has occurred at any time in the last 15 million years. ...We're on track for a 4°C warmer world marked by extreme heat-waves, declining global food stocks, loss of ecosystems and biodiversity, and life-threatening sea level rise."[9]

"By changing the temperature balance between the Arctic and mid-latitudes, rapid Arctic warming is altering the course of the jet stream, which steers weather systems from west to east around the hemisphere. The Arctic has been warming about twice as fast as the rest of the Northern Hemisphere... Climate change is increasing the likelihood of extreme weather events, such as droughts, storms and floods. The average number of such natural disasters more than doubled from 132 a year over 1980–1985 to 357 over 2005–2009. Although it is hard to link any single disaster directly to climate change... science links global warming to their increased incidence. "[10]

"An example of a recent extreme heat wave is the Russian heat wave of 2010, which had very significant adverse consequences. Preliminary estimates ...put the death toll at 55,000, annual crop failure at about 25 percent, burned areas at more than 1 million hectares, and economic losses at about US$15 billion (1 percent gross domestic product (GDP)) .... The 2012 drought in the United States impacted about 80 percent of agricultural land, making it the most severe drought since the 1950s."[11]

"The warming of the atmosphere and oceans is leading to an accelerating loss of ice from the Greenland and Antarctic ice sheets, and this melting could add substantially to sea-level rise in the future.

---

[9] Turn Down the Heat: Why a 4°C Warmer World Must be Avoided (World Bank, 2012) http://climatechange.worldbank.org/sites/default/files/ Turn Down the heat Why a 4 degree centrigrade warmer world must be a voided.pdf

[10] *Human Development Report 2011* (chap2) (UNDP, 2011) - http://www.undp.org/ content/dam/undp/library/corporate/HDR/2011%20Global%20HDR/ English/HDR 2011 EN Chapter2.pdf

[11] Turn Down the Heat, *op. cit.*

Overall, the rate of loss of ice has more than tripled since the 1993–2003 period."[12]

Effects of environmental degradation

Major environmental problems affect health as explained by the UN:[13]

"More than two million deaths and billions of illnesses a year are attributable to water pollution. ...Urban air pollution is responsible for 300,000 – 700,000 deaths annually and creates chronic health problems for many more people."

"Diseases are spread by uncollected garbage and blocked drains; the health risks from hazardous wastes are typically more localized, but often acute. Wastes affect productivity through the pollution of groundwater resources."

RESOURCE SHORTAGE AND PEAK OIL

When the environmental movement first became prominent in the 1960s and 70s, one dominant fear was that we would 'run out' of resources[14] and that this would stop the continued expansion of the economy. As time has gone by, our understanding has become more sophisticated, but the basic issue is now hitting us.

Today all the talk is about 'peak oil' rather than oil running out. In a nutshell, it is that the world's overall supply of oil has or is about to reach its maximum output and will then decline, while demand for oil is still rising. This is probably the reason for the huge spike in oil prices in 2008.

---

[12] Turn Down the Heat, *op. cit.*

[13] United Nations Research Institute for Social Development, Environmental Degradation and Social Integration, Briefing Paper No. 3, World Summit For Social Development, November 1994

[14] see especially, Donella and Dennis Meadows, Jorgen Randers, William Behrents, *The Limits to Growth,* Club of Rome, 1974.

It starts from the observation that every oil field has a limited lifetime. Its oil output rises at first, then peaks and declines. The same is true for all the oil fields in any country put together.

In the USA, oil production peaked in 1970. Before that the USA was an oil exporter. Since then, it has imported larger and larger amounts of oil. The UK had its bonanza of North Sea oil, but that peaked in 1999, and oil output has declined ever since. China's consumption of oil has been growing rapidly but it became a net importer of oil in 2006. Out of the world's 98 oil producing countries, oil output has peaked and started to decline in 64 of them.

> **You** Hasn't that been discredited? There are always stories in the news about new oil fields, and other sources of oil, like tar sands in Canada, vast new gas fields, shale gas, etc.

> **Me** Of course, new oil fields are discovered all the time, and there is a lot of hype by the industry: the new shale oil and gas fields deplete very rapidly, are hugely expensive and polluting. Watch the news over the next year or so!

The world has been very thoroughly explored by now, so new fields being found don't nearly make up for what is running out. The peak in oil discoveries was 1964(!) for the world as a whole. What's worse is that all the places where it is easy to extract the oil have long since been found. The new discoveries are in more difficult places, like deep under the sea bed and so are expensive and dangerous. That means that it takes a lot of energy to get the oil out, meaning that the net energy produced is much lower. The 'energy return on energy invested' (EROI) is falling dramatically. For some newer sources of oil, it may barely be worth the effort.

It looks like the total world output has been at a plateau since around 2006. Many oil producing countries and companies keep their information hidden or distorted for commercial or political reasons, so no objective date is possible.

> **You** So we really are about to run out of oil?

> **Me** No, there is plenty of oil still left. We are running out of *cheap* oil. And it is cheap oil that the global economy relies upon: for

transport, industry, heating, agriculture. Everything we do, really. And that is the problem ...

Other fuels and other resources

Peak oil is the most talked about, but some experts make similar arguments about gas, coal and uranium for nuclear reactors. And also about phosphorus used for fertilisers, and various minerals. As the grade of ore becomes lower, more and more energy is required for extraction. So it isn't just oil that will get more expensive.

HUMANITY AT WAR WITH ITSELF

We can't even make the perverse argument that trashing the planet is helping people to live well. Those parts of humanity with the largest material consumption generally also have little sense of spirituality or community, high mental and emotional instability, unstable families and relationships, high drug use and crime rates, economic insecurity, political corruption and so on. And that is only the richer parts. The poorer parts are beset by wars, poverty, famines, harshly repressive and highly corrupt governments, etc.

To be clearer about how bad the condition of humanity is as a whole, here is a series of quotations from experts who have looked at different aspects of it. The statistics give an impression of the extent of this, but do not convey the full horror, which we can glimpse from the more personal stories we see in television images of genocide and famine.

Wars

"There were 27 major armed conflicts in 1999, there were 11 in Africa, 9 in Asia, 3 in the Middle East, 2 in Europe and 2 in South America. All but two of the conflicts were internal. Most of the major armed conflicts registered for 1999 are protracted (17 have been active for at least eight years) or recurrent (4 conflicts). "[15]

---

[15] *SIPRI Yearbook 2000, Armaments, Disarmament and International Security,* Stockholm International Peace Research Institute.

More recently (2012) there were 9 ongoing wars with annual fatalities greater than 1000, and 30 smaller ones, some of which started as early as the 1940s.[16]

"The USA tops the world's military expenditure at $711 billion, amounting to some 41% of world expenditure. It is followed by China at $143 billion (8.2%)."[17]

"The world total [of military expenditure] for 2011 is estimated to have been $1738 billion, representing 2.5 per cent of global gross domestic product or $249 for each person."[18]

Human rights abuses

"People were tortured and otherwise ill-treated in at least 101 countries, 500,000 people die every year a result of armed violence; millions more are injured, brutally repressed, raped or forced to flee from their homes because of armed conflict, armed violence and human rights violations using conventional arms. 21 of the world's 198 countries carried out executions"[19]

Crime

Crime is endemic all over the world, affecting large proportions of the population. The table below shows the percentage of the population victimised each year in a range of countries.[20]

---

[16] http://en.wikipedia.org/wiki/List_of_ongoing_military_conflicts

[17] *SIPRI Yearbook 2012;* statistics quoted in Wikipedia at http://en.wikipedia.org/wiki/List_of_countries_by_military_expenditures

[18] *SIPRI Yearbook 2012*, Part 2. http://www.sipri.org/yearbook/2012/files/SIPRIYB12Summary.pdf

[19] *Amnesty International Annual Report 2012*, Facts and Figures digest http://files.amnesty.org/air12/fnf_air_2012_en.pdf

[20] Criminal Victimisation in International Perspective: Key findings from the 2004-2005 ICVS and EU ICS - http://rechten.uvt.nl/icvs/pdffiles/ICVS2004_05.pdf

Country	Year	% of Pop	Country	Year	% of pop
Netherlands	2005	19/7	Italy	2005	12.6
England & Wales	2005	21.8	USA	2004	17.5
New Zealand	2004	21.5	Sweden	2005	16.1
Australia	2005	16.3	Mexico	2004	18.7
Switzerland	2005	18.1	Germany	2005	13.1
Scotland	2005	13.3	Belgium	2005	17.7
France	2005	12.0	Finland	2005	12.7
Canada	2004	17.2	Austria	2005	11.6
Spain	2005	9.1	Ireland	2005	21.9
Bulgaria	2004	14.1	Northern Ireland	2005	20.4

The cost of crime is not just the direct costs to the victims, but also includes the cost of running services like the police, customs, courts and prisons.

"Recorded crime in England, Wales and Northern Ireland cost nearly £15 billion in 2007, equivalent to nearly £275 for every person.:[21]

Hunger and poverty

"About 870 million people are estimated to have been undernourished in the period 2010–12. This represents 12.5 percent of the global population, or one in eight people. The vast majority of these – 852 million – live in developing countries, where the prevalence of undernourishment is now estimated at 14.9 percent of the population."[22]

---

[21] Matthew Sinclair & Corin Thompson: 'The Cost of Crime', The Taxpayers' Alliance, 2008

[22] *The State of Food Insecurity in the World 2012*, FAO, http://www.fao.org/publications/sofi/en/

"One in four of the world's children are stunted. In developing countries the proportion can rise to one in three."[23]

"Thirty million people a year die of hunger. And 800 million suffer from chronic malnutrition."[24]

Inequality

"The richest 50 individuals in the world have a combined income greater than that of the poorest 416 million. The 2.5 billion people living on less than $2 a day – 40% of the world's population – receive only 5% of global income, while 54% of global income goes to the richest 10% of the world's population."[25]

Family and emotional problems

The family within a community has traditionally been the basis of human societies. In many countries now, much of the sense of community is gone and even the family is in very poor shape.

[For the United States] "Cherlin compares the likelihood of marrying, divorcing, remarrying and redivorcing of four cohorts of women (born 1908-1912, 1928-1932, 1948-1952, 1970). ...The marriage rates are quite similar [but the] likelihood of divorce is dramatically different for each of these generations. The lifetime chance that the first generation would divorce was 22% while the lifetime probability for the great-granddaughters born in 1970 is 44%."[26]

[23] World Food Programme, https://www.wfp.org/hunger/stats

[24] Ignacio Ramonet, "The politics of hunger", *Le Monde Diplomatique*, November, 1998.

[25] *UNDP Human Development Report 2005*, http://www.stwr.org/poverty-inequality/global-inequality.html

[26] A. Cherlin, *Marriage, Divorce and Remarriage*, (2nd ed.). Cambridge, MA: Harvard University Press, 1992.

"Overall, about 25% of children live in single-parent households. It is also estimated that about 40% of children will EVER live in a single-parent household while they are under 18 years of age."[27]

"40 population-based quantitative studies, conducted in 24 countries on four continents, revealed that between 20% and 50% of the women interviewed reported that they had suffered physical violence from their male partners. In addition, surveys also indicate that at least one in five women suffer rape or attempted rape in their lifetimes."[28]

IS THE GLOBAL CANCER INEVITABLE?

The picture painted so far in this chapter is pretty bleak. No-one could doubt the desirability of dramatically reducing the global cancer. So are these problems intractable, inevitable, inherent in the nature of things? The global cancer often seems inevitable because there are so many interlocking factors that combine to regenerate it. If it were, there would be no point in even thinking about eGaia. The social vision in the previous chapter would be an unattainable fantasy.

The next chapter looks at the dominant role of our economic system (and especially the money system) in creating and perpetuating the global cancer, but let's first look at whether, simply in physical and biological terms, sustainability is possible, given current and future human population levels. And if possible, would it mean either continuing inequality with plenty for a few and poverty for most, or at best a life of great austerity for everyone?

> **You** Surely human population growth is the elephant in the room. There are just too many people.

---

[27] P. C. Glick, (1988). "The role of divorce in the changing family structure: Trends and variations." In S. A. Wolchik & P. Karoly (eds.), *Children of Divorce, Empirical Perspectives on Adjustment.* pp. 3-34). New York: Gardner, 1988.

[28] Executive Summary of the WHO/FIGO Pre-Congress Workshop, Elimination of violence against women 30 – 31 July 1997.

Me World population has tripled in my lifetime. Yes, that is a major reason we are hitting the Earth's limits. And when I was younger it looked like it would rise indefinitely. but that isn't what has been happening.

World population has just passed 7 billion and is still rising, but the rate of increase has peaked and population may stabilise towards the end of the 21st century.

"the global annual increment – that is, the number of people added to the world's population each year – is thought to have peaked between 1985 and 1990 at about 87 million per year."[29]

There is even the possibility that world population overall may reach a maximum and then decline:

"the United Nations Population Division's biennial compendium, World Population Prospects... will include a "low variant" projection that anticipates zero population growth for the world as a whole by the year 2040, and negative growth--that is to say, depopulation--thereafter."[30]

What about energy? Is our use of fossil fuels and nuclear power inevitable? Could renewable energy sources (wind, solar, water, wave energy, etc) produce all of humanity's requirements? Yes, certainly: the technologies are now very well established and are being used more and more. The amount of renewable energy available would be ample on current projections. But the total of humanity's requirements in the future depends upon how our societies are organised. All of humanity could live materially comfortable lives with much lower overall energy use than at present if it were organised collaboratively as in the preceding chapter. The principal obstacles to increased use of renewal energy are economic and social, not technical or physical. We are very fixed in our present social patterns.

---

[29] World Resources Institute, "Population Growth -- Stabilization," at http://www.wri.org/publication/content/8599

[30] Nicholas Eberstadt *What if it's a World Population Implosion?, Speculations about Global De-population,* American Enterprise Institute, Harvard Center for Population and Development Studies, March 1998

Is hunger inevitable, given the size of the Earth's population? It doesn't seem so:

"Food is not in short supply. In fact, food products have never been so abundant. There is enough available to provide each of the Earth's inhabitants with at least 2,700 calories a day. But production alone is not enough. ..."[31]

"...some scientists calculate reassuringly that, with present-day technology put to work on all potentially arable lands, planet Earth could feed fifteen, twenty or even forty billion inhabitants. But rarely does the real world intrude upon theoretical computations wearing such a gaunt face as it does in the case of food."[32]

Hunger is caused by the social patterns that exclude people from the food that is produced and from the land they need to grow their own, not by biological constraints. We certainly don't need another 'Green revolution' in food using, for example, genetically modified plants.

What about other aspects of serious poverty? Are they beyond the scale of what is possible to provide? Not at all.

"The UN calculates that the whole of the world population's basic needs for food, drinking water, education and medical care could be covered by a levy of less than 4% on the accumulated wealth of the 225 largest fortunes. To satisfy all the world's sanitation and food requirements would cost only $13 billion, hardly as much as the people of the United States and the European Union spend each year on perfume."[33]

What is at issue is who gets what and who doesn't, not whether it is physically possible to eliminate poverty. The present system, with people locked into the pressures of financial flows, simply doesn't address the problems of serious poverty.

---

[31] Ignacio Ramonet, "The politics of hunger" *Le Monde Diplomatique*, Nov. 1998.

[32] Erik P. Eckholm, *Losing Ground, Environmental Stress and World Food Prospects,* Pergamon, 1976, p.181.

[33] Ignacio Ramonet, "The politics of hunger" Le Monde Diplomatique, *op. cit.*

And then there is disease. There is a statement earlier in this chapter about the large number of illnesses and deaths that are a by-product of environmental degradation, particularly in poorer countries. Similarly, it is well known that the improvements of the health of populations in the more developed countries in the early 20th century were largely due to better hygiene and living conditions rather than advances in medical science. So again, here is a major problem rooted in social patterns, and certainly not inevitable.

What about wars, and especially the genocides and ethnic cleansings which so marred the 20th century? It is not that the Germans, Serbs, Rwandans, (and now the Israelis) have some gene that makes them particularly bloodthirsty or evil. Rather, when the conditions are right for it, groups of people get caught up in destructive ideas that become self-regenerating within that group, locked in place by powerful emotions. Often it is fears and insecurities arising from difficult economic conditions, which are then turned against some other group of people by demagogic leaders.

These large-scale ethnic conflicts can be seen as diseases of the human spirit. As with physical diseases, it is the underlying social patterns that create the susceptibility – not something innate and inevitable in human nature.

The same arguments apply to all aspects of the global cancer. The conditions under which they are likely are widespread, and so they happen. There is no inevitability about them.

To the extent that societies are organised to do anything about it, the symptoms are usually tackled – often too late to do any good – rather than the conditions that give rise to them. The conditions come from the particular and largely accidental way human societies have developed. They are mostly taken for granted as, for example, our assumption that exchange must be through money.

If we have any hopes of living in a world without the global cancer, we need to be aware and organised to avoid those conditions, but also have strategies for catching them early should they arise. That is the purpose of eGaia.

5 It's the economy, stupid!

"Money is institutionalised mistrust" Professor Mike Hussey

Our ideas about money are illusions, clouding the collective minds of humanity. They are at the heart of why humanity is a cancer of the natural world, and are central to why we are at war with ourselves. Here are some of those illusions:

- The purpose of working is to make money, rather than to serve the community.

- The purpose of business is to make money, and businesses seek to optimise themselves to do so rather than to serve the community.

- The principle way of obtaining goods and services is to buy them with money.

- Money is the main indicator of the value of things.

- *'The bottom line'* is *'what is real'*.

- Prosperity requires economic growth (i.e. growth in monetary transactions) rather than improvement in wellbeing.

- Paying financial debts takes priority over social goals.

All of these are so ingrained in our culture that they are rarely questioned.

> **You** You have come to the conclusion that money is the root of all evil!

> **Me** The actual quote is from the Bible, *(I Tim, VI, 10)*[34] "The love of money is the root of all evil things." But no, I don't agree with it. The root is social and spiritual fragmentation, the loss of connection with the Earth and sense of community between people. Money enables us to carry on dealing with each other despite that. It looms centre stage in the global cancer but is not at its root.

---

[34] *The New English Bible*, 1970.

And let's be clear that it is this 'clouding of our collective minds' that needs to change. It won't work to declare that the rich are evil and need to be removed, and that all will be well if that happens.

OUR UPSIDE DOWN ECONOMY

To be clear about why our economy is so central to the global cancer, we can contrast it with the economic system in the fictional story in Chapter 3. In the story, the change came about as a result of a collapse of the global money system, which forced people to let go of their illusions about it.

With that came the realisation that the money system is not the real economy. Without money, we are still left with all the farms, factories, trucks and ships, with all the people who want to receive and who want to contribute to their communities. This is the *real economy*: those activities where people make things and do things for one another. The function of the money system is no more than to enable them to come to agreement (and often not a willing agreement) about who gets what and who does what, but the money system has taken on a life of its own and now dominates the real economy. When people think the economy is in trouble, they are mostly thinking about the money system.

The money system enables us to deal with strangers with whom we have no ongoing relationship. It provides justifications for forcing people to do things they don't want to do.

In the story, change was driven by people with little money and large needs and with the shadow of a deteriorating natural world hanging over them. Out of desperation, they set up new co-operative enterprises in their communities whose goals were to serve those needs, taking the environment into account. This was the key change.

    You The key change was the goals?

    Me Yes, this is one of the most important points I am trying to make in this book. If the goal of an organisation is to serve some aspect of the wellbeing of people and planet directly, it can be optimised for that, with all thinking and resources devoted to that. If the goal is to make money, and an organisation is optimised for that, it turns the economy upside down! Everything is done for the wrong reasons. When I hear proposals to reform some aspect of the money system that leave this fundamental issue untouched, I always think how limited it is.

To take an example, compare the farm and sustainable supermarket in the story with today's farms and supermarkets. Today's supermarkets are not about optimising the distribution of the most nourishing and environmentally sustainable food, they are themed marketing opportunities. Once the customer is there, it makes sense to sell anything that makes the most money. Highly processed foods and junk foods have higher profit margins even if they are unhealthy. It makes financial sense to encourage people to buy more than they need with special offers, to fly food in from all over the world regardless of the energy it takes, to sell the most profitable lines of clothing, appliances, electronics, even though it puts a full service local shop out of business. Optimising for profit is very different from optimising for wellbeing.

Most of our productive effort is now through paid work, motivated largely by our need for money. It is a nice side benefit if your job is beneficial to your community or to the planet. If it gives you prestige and social standing, that is a luxury for some rather than the immediate and direct motivation for that work. The global economy is driven by money flows, not wellbeing or need. This is a major source of our environmental problems and social problems.

The best companies try to put their customers' needs first, but even then there is an underlying conflict. They want and need you to patronise them, even if it really isn't in your best interests to do so. Huge amounts of productive work are devoted to encouraging people to want more of something. Shopping has become one of our most popular leisure activities. Governments encourage their citizens to consume more.[35]

---

[35] for example, the Japanese government gave out vouchers to encourage people to consume. J. Watts, "Even free money fails to tempt Japan's shoppers", *The Guardian*, 1 Feb. 1999.

We are told we must increase production – not so much because the public is in desperate need of digital TVs, the next generation of computers or a new theme park, much less because we need to preserve the health of the environment – but because we need to produce more to safeguard jobs. Consumption serves production, not the other way round.

As money became the dominant mechanism of exchange, the connection with real needs and desires became looser. It has become highly abstract, with money flows taking on a life of their own. Survival for an enterprise has come to depend upon maintaining the flows of money. Bankruptcy generally means the end of an organisation, regardless of whether it is corrupt or dedicated to the public good. Charities need to maintain their cash flows to survive too.

This creates an inherent contradiction between the need for an organisation to survive and any other goals, such as serving the public or looking after your staff. The 'bottom line', the effect on the financial balance sheet is widely used to mean 'that which is real, undeniable'. In fact, it is just a convention, an artefact of the way we organise ourselves economically. In a co-operative economy the only 'bottom line' is everybody's wellbeing.

If you look around and notice activities that seem absurd or antisocial or that harm the natural world, it is usually because someone's goal is to make money rather than to serve society:

- A rainforest can be cut down for short-term economic gain because its vital biological contribution has no economic value.
- An airport or a railway station becomes a shopping mall, trying to extract as much money as possible from the people who use it.
- Television channels appear that are fully dedicated to advertising, with no programme content at all.
- Companies produce new versions of solid, useful well-loved, well-understood products and convince consumers that the old ones are obsolete or old-fashioned.

But that is just the start. In many 'legitimate' activities people are actually preying on people rather than serving them: making and selling shoddy goods, junk email and phone calls.

Easily the worst is corruption and crime, organised or casual. It is endemic, not because there are lots of greedy and evil people, but because in our upside-down economy, it is money and not service that drives people's actions. In traditional societies crime is quite rare and tends to be mostly to do with interpersonal conflict.

> "Corruption diverts perhaps 30 percent from billions of dollars spent annually for international development loans. Importantly, this illegitimate cash flow becomes the primary reason why funds are requested."[36]

> "By most estimates, the traffic in illicit drugs is one of the world's most substantial money earners. The retail value of drugs, at around 500 billion US dollars a year, now exceeds the value of the international trade in oil and is second only to that of the arms trade."[37]

>> **You** So two of the world's largest industries are the arms trade and the illegal drugs trade?

>> **Me** So it would seem. How's that for an upside-down economy?

WHAT IS WRONG WITH OUR MONEY SYSTEM?

The history of money is not a happy one. From the start it was intimately connected with war and slavery, as will be explained in Part 2 of eGaia. The problems we now face have a long history, but have grown particularly severe in the past few decades, with globalisation and financial deregulation. In recent years, and especially since the 2008 financial crisis,

---

[36] Richard G. Dudley, "The Rotten Mango: The Effect of Corruption on International Development Projects", Eighteenth International Conference of the System Dynamics Society "*Sustainability in the Third Millennium*". August 6-10, 2000. Bergen, Norway.

[37] *Illicit Drugs: Social Impacts and Policy Responses,* UNRISD Briefing Paper No. 2 World Summit For Social Development November 1994

there has been a huge amount written about how dysfunctional it is.[38] In this chapter, I will only pick a few of the main arguments that are relevant to the eGaian vision.

In the fictional story in Chapter 3 there was a new money system, created largely after the fictional crash. It was used primarily as a medium of exchange between people where there wasn't an ongoing relationship of trust. The supply of money was controlled by the community that used it and expanded and contracted as needed. It was never scarce. Unlike today's money system, it did not dominate and distort trade. And also, a lot was done without money at all within the local community, between people with ongoing relationships.

In contrast to this, our present global money system shares with the rest of the economy the wrong goals: it is organised to make money out of money, not to serve the needs of humanity.

Thomas Greco lists three principal ways in which our money system malfunctions:[39]

1. Money is kept artificially scarce, so there is never enough to serve the purposes for which it is created.

2. Money is misallocated at its source, going to those with power not need.

3. The money system systematically pumps wealth from the poor and middle classes to the rich.

Historically, money was created by governments, often to pay for wars, and the common view of money is that this is still the case. But it is no longer true:

---

[38] For example, Chris Martenson, *The Crash Course: The Unsustainable Future Of Our Economy, Energy, And Environment,* John Wiley & Sons, 317pp, or online at http://www.peakprosperity.com/crashcourse, or see http://www.positivemoney.org/

[39] Thomas H. Greco, Jr. *Money, Understanding and Creating Alternatives to Legal Tender,* Chelsea Green, 2001.

"The essence of the contemporary monetary system is creation of money out of nothing, by private banks' often foolish lending."[40]

Almost all of the money in circulation is created when a bank gives a loan, just by the act of adding that sum to the receiver's bank account. The money isn't taken from other bank holdings. New money simply comes into existence. This gives the banks extraordinary power.

When money is created as a loan, the terms of repayment usually include interest. This is not inherent in the nature of loans. In earlier times, lending money for interest was called usury and wasn't allowed. There are modern examples of lending where there is a transaction fee to cover costs, but no interest.[41]

This is one of the major mechanisms for the systematic transfer of wealth to the already wealthy. It is also the real reason why economic growth is needed! Without it, loans cannot be repaid because there isn't enough money overall.

> **You** So the need for economic growth is just an artefact of the money system!
>
> **Me** You've got it. The real economy could remain stable if the money system were different. In the fictional story, there is no need for growth. Work is there to satisfy needs and provide wellbeing.

The money system is one of our biggest 'industries'. Making money out of money doesn't require factories, transport, or resources so it can appear to be an easy way to make money. Although it is not part of the productive real economy, banks and other organisations use the language of business to sell 'financial products'. Markets were once places where goods changed hands. Now, 'the market' often refers to currency, stock and commodity markets where what is actually being sold is money and debt: ownership of

---

[40] Martin Wolf, *Financial Times*, 9th November 2010

[41] This is the case with Islamic banks, or the Swedish JAK co-operative bank, for example.

a company, a future contract to buy a physical product, or perhaps a package of loans put together to reduce risk.

As these are abstractions, not physical, they are completely separated from physical and social reality, especially in the minds of the market traders. What matters is whether a trade makes a profit, not how it affects people or the planet.

As a result, these financial markets are inherently highly unstable. Traders may buy something because they think other traders think its value will rise so they can make a profit, even if this has no real basis.

> "Between 1970 and 2010 a total of 425 financial crises affecting member states of the International Monetary Fund was officially recorded: 145 banking crises, 208 monetary crashes and 72 sovereign-debt crises."[42]

There have been many financial 'bubbles' where values have risen outrageously and then collapsed, such as the tulip mania in the 1630s, the South Sea Bubble in 1720, the Great Depression of the 1930s, and the Dotcom Bubble of the 1990s. When they collapse, they often take the real economy with them.

After the Great Depression, many governments imposed stringent regulations on banks and other financial organisations, hoping to avoid a repeat. However, the pressure to make more money from money was always strong, and by the 1980s, with the rise to power of Ronald Reagan and Margaret Thatcher, the fashion changed once again to deregulation. This, combined with the IT revolution, led to an unprecedented growth in the financial system, as compared to the real economy.

---

[42] Bernard Lietaer, et al. *Money and Sustainability. The Missing Link.* Axminster: Triarchy Press, 2012.

The result was what Tim Morgan calls "a 'credit super-cycle', which can be regarded as 'the biggest bubble in history'."[43] It ended with the credit crunch of 2008, and we are still living with the results.

IS A CRASH OF THE MONEY SYSTEM LIKELY?

In the fictional story in Chapter 3, the breakthrough came about in the aftermath of a crash of the money system.

> **You** Do you think a crash of the money system is desirable?
>
> **Me** No. I would like to see a rapid, managed transition to the kind of eGaian society I describe in the story. It would be far better for it to come about through people taking up the new vision and letting go of the old. But I do think a crash is very likely because that change of vision is happening very slowly and the old ideas are very entrenched. However, the transition needs to occurs before runaway global warming really takes hold, if it hasn't already.

The difficulties with the money system now are different than at any time in the past. This current debt bubble is much larger than any previous one, so the instability in the money system is much worse than ever. With all the interconnections, if a crash begins it is likely to be unstoppable.

And a crash is more likely to be triggered now, because we are reaching the Earth's limits, as described in the last chapter. For example, extreme weather events are putting a huge strain on the global economy.

But it is peak oil, as described in the previous chapter, that will be putting the greatest strain on the money system. In the absence of the kind of low energy economy described in the fictional story, the demand for energy will continue to rise, while its supply becomes limited and much more expensive. It was probably the cause of the spike in oil prices in 2008 that triggered the Credit Crunch.

---

[43] Tim Morgan, *Perfect storm, energy, finance and the end of growth,* 2013, http://tullettprebonresearch.com/2012/12/20/the-economy-at-the-cliff-edge-our-new-report/

Without growth in energy, economic growth cannot continue. Without economic growth, debts cannot be paid, and so the whole unstable house of cards will collapse.

Tim Morgan points out five markers to watch for:

"Energy price escalation ...chokes off economic growth and imposes short-term reverses in demand.

Agricultural stress ... more frequent spikes in food prices, combined with food shortfalls in the poorest countries.

Energy sprawl. Investment in the energy infrastructure will absorb a steadily-rising proportion of global capital investment.

Economic stagnation ... the world economy can be expected to become increasingly sluggish.

Inflation."[44]

> **You** What lessons do you take from this?

> **Me** The most important is to keep clear about what is real: the real economy is not the money system. It is not the banks that need to be protected, it is people and vital services. Debts are not sacrosanct. Large scale cancellation of debts of all kinds is a good idea as Iceland has demonstrated!

---

[44] Tim Morgan, *op. cit.*

6 eGaian principles

We've looked at an eGaian vision of the future and compared it with the global cancer that is today's society. Now it is time to pull the threads together.

Three basic principles

Three overall principles characterise an eGaian world and follow directly from the analysis of the global cancer.

1. *Peace.*. People come to see all humanity as part of their extended family, accepting and appreciating the differences between cultures. They add to their sense of identity a strong sense of being part of humanity and a concern for its overall wellbeing. Human activities are organised to take into account the needs of other groups and co-ordinate with them, rather than compete with them. To make this possible, the basic human communication skills of seeing from another's perspective, appreciating human differences, coming to agreement, and especially handling conflict would be seen as the most basic and fundamental

parts of human culture. Conflict resolution would be as natural a social technology as growing food.

2. *Sustainability* Looking after the health of the natural world – the whole of the living Earth – becomes a primary value for all of humanity. So human activities are organised with that in mind.

3. *The right goals.* The direct pursuit of peace, human wellbeing and sustainability replace our current goals of pursuit of profit and financial survival (with human wellbeing as its supposed side-benefit). This transforms much of the economic and political structure of the world. The basic social organising principle is to be aware of the core goals and to act to correct errors, or deviations from them. What could be more simple or direct? In engineers' terms, it means society is organised as an error-correcting, feedback control system with its goals the wellbeing of the whole.

HUMANITY AS A GLOBAL NERVOUS SYSTEM

If humanity with its current huge population and dominance takes on this role of caring for the Earth-as-a-whole, the result is that it would come to have a coherence and a wholeness it has never had. In that respect it would become like a single, global-scale organism.[45]

The Earth now lacks the wholeness and coherence which characterise those things we currently call organisms. The coherence of an organism goes along with a greatly reduced role for competition between its parts and much more mutual support. When an itchy scalp results in a hand scratching it, that is a highly co-ordinated, co-operative response by billions of cells. A large-scale global effort to relieve a famine or Earthquake damage in one country has something of the same character.

The point of the three fundamental eGaian principles above is to spread that kind of support and co-ordination to all aspects of human life, and

---

[45] Peter Russell has been developing this image for a long time. See his *The Awakening Earth, Our Next Evolutionary Leap*, Routledge & Kegan Paul, London, 1982.

beyond – to the natural world. Such a change would mark a major step in the evolution of life on Earth. Through its evolutionary history, the scale of the coherence of life has increased from that of the first microbes, to complex cells, to multi-cellular forms, to organisms like plants and animals. Extending that coherence to the whole planet could be the next step in that progression.

The mechanism for the social process that would create global scale coherence is communication and information processing. The function of humanity would be analogous to a nervous system. An animal with a nervous system is an error-correcting feedback control system with the nervous system as its communication and information processing system. A nervous system is as much controlled by its body as vice versa. It is part of the body and responds to its needs. Thus when you scratch that itch, the nervous system first has to notice the discomfort and send signals about that to the brain (feedback). Comparing the signal (itching) to the desired state (no itching) shows there is an error. The nervous system then determines the action required and sends signals through the nerves in the arm and muscles to activate the movements needed (the error-correcting control).

Similarly, creating a globally-coherent Earth would involve humanity becoming integrated within it. Humanity would respond to the needs of the Earth rather than trying to control it for its own purposes. For humanity to look after the health of the natural world, it has to monitor its state, work out where action is needed and act accordingly. For humanity to look after its own health, it has to monitor and understand that, going beyond the differences in perspective of different groups, and act accordingly.

COULD IT HAPPEN?

The growing connections between people through IT and social media is just one of the changes that underpins an eGaian future. It is only during the past century – through films, radio and TV – that people have seen into each other's cultures on a mass scale. People everywhere can now identify with the victims of famine and war anywhere. An eGaian culture would require us to move beyond the culture-bound blindnesses of our past. We are only now reaching the point where we can build a sense of identity as part of the global human species rather than as part of one culture competing with the rest.

In the past few decades we have been able to see the Earth from space, to give us a sense of the Earth as home to us all. Now the living Earth and the threats to it are becoming understood. At the same time as our population has burgeoned and our technology has increased its impact, our scientists have become able to monitor the damage we are doing. Global warming, holes in the ozone layer, loss of habitats and species, air and water pollution are now routinely taught in schools. Children are many of our most committed environmentalists.

During the last century we developed an understanding of feedback, stability, control and their use in self-regulating systems. These ideas inform our understanding of how organisms and ecosystems maintain their form and health. As we have developed machines that communicate, the theory of communication has grown with it. Studies of human psychology have teased out important principles of how we make sense of the world and how we form our sense of self. It is only through the conscious application of these ideas that we can replace our destructive expansion with a stable, self-regulating culture.

This powerful cocktail of ideas, together with the technical means of communication, gives us the opportunity to create self-aware, stable, self-organising social structures based upon co-operation and community. The image of eGaia can provide pointers in the direction of that future. It can generate guidelines for ways to behave, ways to live sustainably and in harmony with each other. This can provide the 'shoulds' and 'oughts' which science, as we know it now, cannot. These turn out to be the same at a deep level as some of the teachings of the ancient religions, but without the need to appeal to ancient authority.

The image of eGaia builds upon the earliest spiritual imagery of humanity: Gaia, the Mother Earth goddess. It can provide a sense of being part of a larger whole and also a sense of purpose. Many people share large parts of this vision (and it resonates with many traditional cultures). Huge numbers are seeking ways of living more sustainably. Many are looking for co-operative, community-based ways of living. The ether is thick with new forms of spirituality, many based on a regained harmony with nature.

PART 2 CONTEXT: THE FIVE BILLION YEAR STORY

7 Symbiosis and competition: the story of life on Earth

"We are symbionts on a symbiotic planet, and if we care to, we can find symbiosis everywhere." Lynn Margulies[46]

You: Why is this chapter needed?

Me: This chapter is much longer and more detailed than is needed for the core message of eGaia. I actually researched and wrote the first version of it a few years before I wrote *eGaia*. I have left it in fully because a) changing our sense of nature as inherently competitive is vital if we are to create a collaborative society, and b) I think it is a great story. I love it, and hope you will be fascinated by it too. But skip it if it doesn't grab you!

---

46 Lynn Margulies, *The Symbiotic Planet, A New Look at Evolution*, Basic Books, 1998.

We complex living beings are composed of organs and tissues, which in turn are composed of cells, in turn of molecules, in turn atoms, and so on. Each organ has its symbiotic place in the organism, each species has its niche in the web of life. It is all one great co-operative dance. The Hindus call it the dance of Shiva. In the Middle Ages in Europe it was seen as the harmony of life. The story of life and its evolution is a mixture of symbiosis – living together – and competition.

With the rise of the competitive market economy and later the Darwinian theory of evolution, the competitive side of the story of life came to be emphasised out of all proportion to its contribution. We now see nature as 'red in tooth and claw' with only the fittest (often taken to mean strongest) surviving at the expense of the others. This image is consistent with our view of the economy. Companies compete to survive, with the weak going out of business. Similarly, in politics, parties compete in a parliamentary democracy. The strongest, the majority parties, get to impose their views on the minority.

This consistency across our views of nature, economics and politics adds to a sense that it is all for the best and inevitable. Of course we should have a competitive economy and a competitive political system. That is the way of nature.

But this belief is actually very destructive. It is part of the pattern by which the global cancer regenerates itself. To show that the global cancer is not actually a law of nature requires a different view of nature. The prospect of a genuinely co-operative economy, based upon symbiosis and niche-filling is not on many people's agenda. Neither is a politics where differences are respected and a consensus sought which best satisfies those different views. But these are consistent with the view of nature that is described in this chapter. The story of life is about the interplay of symbiosis and competition. Competition does have a role to play, but it is only part of the story. In a multi-cellular organism, competition between the cells is actively suppressed in favour of symbiosis. In a co-operative society, competition between ideas remains very important, but not the kinds of competition which today lead to poverty and the suppression of minorities.

In order to build a co-operative society we will need new metaphors for what is natural. This chapter builds on the metaphors of recycling and of co-ordination of parts in an organism.

A second important message that will come out of this evolutionary story is the warning lesson from the major extinctions of the past, and there were several in the past few billion years. Each time, a large percentage of the Earth's living creatures died and many species went extinct. These were associated with changes in climate, very much of the sort which humanity is now triggering as one of the side effects of the global cancer.

BEFORE LIFE: THE HADEAN AGE

The Earth formed out of a spinning cloud of dust about 5 billion years ago. Most of that dust settled at the centre of the cloud and formed the Sun. The material of the Sun – mostly hydrogen – contracted and became hotter until the Sun ignited in a thermonuclear reaction that continues today. The remainder of the cloud (only a fraction of a per cent of the total), dispersed over hundreds of millions of miles, settled into a disk, and then into clumps. The largest of these clumps formed the nine major planets – Mercury, Venus, Earth, Mars, Jupiter, Saturn, Uranus, Neptune, and Pluto, spinning around the Sun in elliptical orbits.

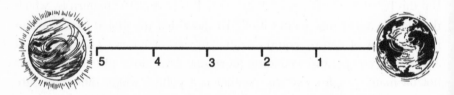

Billion years ago...

The Sun is far too hot for anything solid to form. The planets are too small to burn like the Sun. For the complex molecules that make up life to form, the right materials had to be present, under the right conditions. The outer planets were always far too cold. The innermost planets – Mercury and Venus – were probably always too hot. Earth and Mars were the only two which ever came close.

The conditions on the early Earth were totally unlike the present. Much of the surface was volcanic and the surface was too hot to allow any oceans. Any rain that hit the surface boiled away immediately. The atmosphere was largely carbon dioxide, like Mars and Venus today. Oxygen, so vital to life now, wasn't there. The present conditions on Earth co-evolved with life over the billions of years since. Life has not been a passive passenger on Earth, but has been a major shaper and maintainer of the conditions it needed.

The Hadean Age

This period before life is called the Hadean Age[47] and fits well with the classical images of Hell. Eventually, the Earth cooled until its surface temperature dropped below the boiling point of water. The rains fell for millions of years and the seas were formed. The earliest sedimentary rocks date from this time.

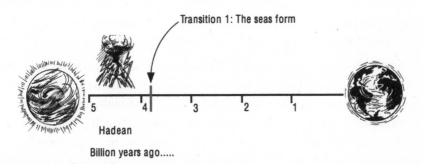

Transition 1: The seas form

5   4   3   2   1

Hadean

Billion years ago.....

[47] Lynn Margulies and Dorian Sagan, *Microcosmos, Four Billion Years of Microbial Evolution*, Allen and Unwin, 1987, p.47.

FIRST LIFE: THE ARCHEAN AGE

When the seas had formed and the Earth was cool enough, conditions soon became suitable for the formation of the earliest forms of life. And life did form almost as soon as it became possible – within a few hundred million years.

You You call a few hundred million years soon?

Me On these time scales, yes.

Those early seas are what we call the 'primordial soup'. The seas and the atmosphere contained molecules that were simple combinations of hydrogen, oxygen, nitrogen and sulphur that later came to make up most of the components of life. Local micro-environments formed where conditions were more stable and in which larger molecules could form. Simpler molecules were continually forming more complex molecules and breaking up again to form simpler molecules, their links forged and destroyed by the energy of the Sun. For example, molecules of hydrogen cyanide (one hydrogen atom, one carbon atom and one nitrogen atom – HCN) could form a chain by connecting to itself five times. The result is adenine ($H_5C_5N_5$), one of the main components of the genetic material, DNA.

Some of these molecules turned out to be catalysts: they acted as templates on which other molecules assembled to form larger, more complex molecules. In effect, the template formed a map of the structure of the molecule it helped to form With a template, the molecule could assemble much more readily.

Chains of reactions began, where the results of some reactions were the starting materials for other reactions, whose results were the starting materials for still other reactions, and so on. Eventually, some chains of reactions appeared which were closed: the results of the last reaction were the starting materials needed for the first one, so the chain could start again. By this point, life was not far away. The other necessary component for life was the membrane: a molecular net with holes that allowed some materials through and blocked others. The earliest of these were simple repeated assemblies of molecules, formed by chains of molecules sticking to each other.

Molecules, closed chain reactions and membranes are the elements of a rudimentary cell. This was the forerunner of today's bacteria, and the basis of all later life[48]. Those first cells can be seen as the beginnings of symbiosis on a molecular level. Each component was needed for the continuation of the others.

There is much more to the story before a bacteria-like cell appeared, but that is the start of it. The membrane had to allow in any raw materials not created by the cycle of reactions and allow out any by-products not used in them. The templates had to be able to re-form not only themselves but also the membrane. The whole had to be sufficiently robust so as to be able to re-form itself against damage caused by the continually changing micro-environment.

You So that's the secret of life! Are you sure about all this?

Me No, but it's the best we can do. Almost none of it is based on direct evidence. It comes from a combination of laboratory experiments, mathematical and computer simulations, and a lot of theoretical speculation. It is all other people's work, and the details of it are way beyond my understanding. There are great gaps in it, but it seems plausible. More important, the patterns and processes I've been describing here are similar to others which will appear later in the book. I'm hoping to show you a grand pattern, whose consistency on many levels will add to its overall plausibility.

These primitive cells show a whirlpool-like pattern – a form that is continually re-formed from a surrounding sea of its parts. With a cell, however, there is an important extra – the templates: the genetic material, the RNA and DNA, which appears in every cell in all living creatures. They provide a description of the essentials of the structure of the cell. It is

---

[48] This is an area of knowledge that has changed a lot recently. Now the earliest life are seen as bacteria and archaea, which are similar simple cells, but are much less well known than bacteria. In what follows what I say about bacteria really should say bacteria and archaea.

that description that gives the cell the coherence that maintains its wholeness. The information in that description is crucial to the maintenance of the form of the cell. As we will see later in the book, it is similar to the use of information and communications to maintain the form of a co-operative eGaian society.

THE SYMBIOTIC BACTERIAL LIFESTYLE

The earliest forms of life developed from primitive proto-bacteria to full bacteria over an extended period following the formation of the seas, and it was still longer before any more complex life evolved. This period, when bacteria were the only form of life, is called the *Archean*, meaning ancient or beginning.

Bacteria are very simple cells; plant and animal cells are much more complex, with a separate nucleus where most of the genetic material is contained, internal membranes, and numerous small internal structures called organelles. Plant and animal cells also reproduce differently from bacteria. To understand the development of these more complex cells, we first have to look more closely at the life of bacteria.

> **You** Just a minute. Surely bacteria are either plants or animals? Are you saying they are something different?
>
> **Me** Yes. The old idea that life falls into two kingdoms – plants and animals – is now obsolete. There are many creatures that do not fit comfortably into those two categories. The modern division is between cells with and without a nucleus. Those without are the bacteria. They evolved first, in the Archean, nearly 4 billion years ago. Plants, animals and fungi came very much later, less than 500 million years ago.

A bacterium contains a minimal set of genetic material, barely more than needed to re-form itself and reproduce. Yet bacteria are extremely adaptable. They can survive an amazing range of environments – nearly boiling waters, airless conditions, and environments that would be poisonous to any other creatures. They adapt rapidly to changes in their environment, as is clear from the way they have developed resistance to many antibiotics. How does this happen? Margulies and Sagan give a vivid description[49]:

"Its minimal number of genes leaving it deficient in metabolic abilities, a bacterium is necessarily a team player. A bacterium never functions as a single individual in nature. Instead, in any given ecological niche, teams of several kinds of bacteria live together, responding to and reforming the environment, aiding each other with complementary enzymes. The various kinds of bacteria in the team, each present in enormous numbers of copies, co-ordinate the release of their enzymes according to the stages in a task. Their life cycles interlock, the waste products of one kind becoming the food sources of the next. In huge and changing numbers, they perform tasks of which individually they are incapable."

So bacteria can be seen as inherently symbiotic creatures. Living together is an essential part of their lifestyle. This resembles the complementary nature of the reactions within each bacterium, with different reactions contributing materials needed by others and using the results of others.

In bacteria, reproduction and sex are completely separate. A bacterium reproduces by growing to twice its normal size, when its single strand of DNA duplicates itself and the cell splits into two identical cells. The daughter cells are genetically identical to the single parent (which no longer exists).

Sex is the exchange of genetic material. Many mechanisms are available for this. Two bacteria may combine into one, which ends up with all the genetic material. Or bacteria may exchange genetic material through a small tube that forms temporarily to join them (called conjugation). Also, small bits of genetic material may get packaged up in various ways and travel between bacteria. These packages include plasmids, phages and viruses. Viruses, which can be so deadly to creatures with complex nucleated cells like us, are not a separate form of life, but a normal part of the sexual repertoire of bacteria.

---

[49] Lynn Margulies and Dorian Sagan, *op. cit.* p. 71.

In plants and animals, the genetic material in one generation is very much like that in the previous generation. The form of successive generations changes very little within any species. Bacteria are much more fluid. They are continually changing their form and their genetic material, often very radically. This is how resistance to drugs can develop so rapidly.

You Why this prurient interest in the sex lives of bacteria?

Me You may joke, but this is a crucial point. One of the aims of this chapter is to squash the idea that competition is the basic organising principle of nature. It's clear already that to explain the behaviour of bacteria in terms of competition is to leave out most of what is significant.

The lives of bacteria are totally interconnected and interdependent. Their response to changing conditions is that of a group. By modifying the mixture of metabolisms available they adapt as needed. Because of their genetic fluidity, there is a sense in which all the bacteria on Earth can be viewed as a single species; because of their group interdependence, they can even be viewed as a single, global super-organism[50]. To see individual bacteria competing with each other is to misunderstand the nature of their lives. An individual bacterium's fitness to survive depends upon the adaptability of the local colony of bacteria around it.

The earliest bacterial colonies fed on the most readily available molecules in the primordial soup – carbohydrates and alcohols. This is the metabolism of a fermenter. These early forms of metabolism are still with us in the modern bacteria that make our cheese and wine and which live in the guts of most animals and form a vital part of the animals' digestive system. There were many different forms of fermenter, with different metabolisms. In any colony, one fermenter's waste was another's food, so that the basic materials were recycled. Recycling and re-use of materials has been a basic principle of life from the start.

As the early bacterial colonies grew and spread, more and more of the available materials became incorporated into their bodies. Over time, many

---

[50] Sorin Sonea and Maurice Panisset, *The New Bacteriology*, Boston, Jones and Bartlett, 1983, p.22

new metabolic pathways were developed enabling spreading life to eat up more and more of the primordial soup. There must have been many local crises, where no more soup was available and colonies died out. There must also have been many times when, under this pressure, a new metabolic pathway was discovered, and a new source of food allowed the colony to continue. Through the Archean age, nearly all the metabolic pathways used by bacteria today evolved, and these are the building blocks of the metabolisms of all the more complex forms of life.

One particularly important metabolism was photosynthesis, in which sunlight was the energy source. The earliest photosynthetic bacteria were sulfur breathers. They gave off hydrogen sulfide (the gas which gives rotten eggs their smell). A later form of photosynthesizer used carbon dioxide gas, which was abundant in the air and dissolved in the surface of the early seas. Carbon dioxide and water itself provided most of the materials needed. These bacteria extracted carbon from carbon dioxide and hydrogen from water and used them to build the molecules they needed, giving off oxygen as their waste product. Thus the major metabolic pathway used by all modern plants had arrived.

This was a key breakthrough for life. It had resolved its first major crisis. Life had eaten up most of the primordial soup, but could now continue to grow with carbon dioxide as its food.

> **You** Are you saying that photosynthetic bacteria replaced all the others?

Me Not at all. Remember interdependence, interconnectedness and recycling. All the others could continue too.

This was the beginning of the dramatic changes life was to make to the Earth. It had eaten up the soup, turning it into bacteria, and was now beginning to change the atmosphere. The long process of change had begun, from an atmosphere composed mostly of carbon dioxide to today's atmosphere which contains only 0.04% carbon dioxide. This time also marked the first great environmental crisis to hit life.

Today, we hear about carbon dioxide as a greenhouse gas; its increase leading to global warming. In the late Archean age carbon dioxide levels fell and the world cooled, to give the first ice age. This event is a rough marker of the end of the Archean age and the beginning of the Proterozoic.

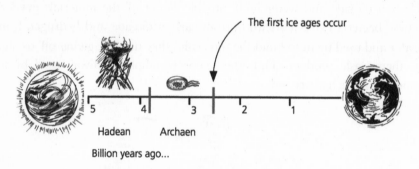

The first ice ages roughly mark the end of the Archean age

Life in the late Archean / early Proterozoic age

"To a casual observer, the early Proterozoic world would have looked largely flat and damp, an alien yet familiar landscape, with volcanoes smoking in the background and shallow, brilliantly colored pools abounding and mysterious greenish and brownish patches of scum floating on the waters, stuck to the banks of rivers, tinting the damp soils like fine molds. A ruddy sheen would coat the stench-filled waters.

Shrunk to microscopic perspective, a fantastic landscape of bobbing purple, aquamarine, red, and yellow spheres would come into view. Inside the violet spheres of *Thiocapsa*, suspended yellow globules of sulfur would emit bubbles of skunky gas. Colonies of ensheathed viscous organisms would stretch to the horizon. One end stuck to rocks, the other ends of some bacteria would insinuate themselves inside tiny cracks and begin to penetrate the rock itself. Long skinny filaments would leave the pack of their brethren, gliding by slowly, searching for a better place in the sun. Squiggling bacterial whips shaped like corkscrews or fusili pasta would dart by. Multicellular filaments and tacky, textilelike crowds of bacterial cells would wave with the currents, coating pebbles with brilliant shades of red, pink, yellow, and green. Showers of spores, blown by breezes, would splash and crash against the vast frontier of low-lying muds and waters."[51]

COMPLEX CELLS: THE PROTEROZOIC AGE

Early photosynthetic bacteria gave off oxygen as well as taking in carbon dioxide. Oxygen was not present in significant quantities in the early atmosphere. It is too reactive: it combined so readily with many other substances that it did not persist as free oxygen. For a long time, rocks rapidly absorbed the oxygen produced by the early photosynthesisers. Some ancient banded iron rocks containing layers of iron oxide have been found, which are evidence for this process.

Eventually, the oxygen given off by bacteria was more than could be absorbed, and it began to build up in the atmosphere. While to us oxygen is vital and a key to life, to the bacteria in the late Archean it was a deadly poison. The reactivity of oxygen destroyed cells. The build-up of oxygen in the late Archean was the greatest pollution crisis life on Earth has ever faced.

Major crises require radical solutions. The outcome of the oxygen crisis was the development of the eukaryotic cell – a new compound cell with a

---

[51] Margulies and Sagan, *op. cit.*, p.97

nucleus. Those cells now form the basis of all animals and plants. Their development marked the major division in life forms.

How did it happen? As oxygen began to accumulate in the Earth's atmosphere, and also dissolved in the sea waters, certain bacteria evolved which, rather than being killed by it, made good use of it. Some forms of *cyanobacteria*, one of the early photosynthesizers, learned the trick of using oxygen in a form of internal, controlled combustion as a source of energy. This was the beginning of respiration. These bacteria could take in oxygen and give off carbon dioxide. This trick not only protected *cyanobacteria* from the ravages of oxygen, it was also a very efficient form of metabolism compared with that of the earlier fermenters. *Cyanobacteria* thrived. Many new oxygen-using forms developed from them. They quickly replaced the oxygen-sensitive bacteria on the oxygen-rich surface, while other bacteria survived underneath them in the lower levels of mud and water.

The stage was also now set for the development of the compound cell. It is known that small bacteria can live independently yet symbiotically inside larger cells. The smaller bacteria find plentiful food inside the host, and their metabolism contributes to that of the host. In some cases, the invader might have started as a predator. Some hosts did not die, and developed not a resistance, but a need for their new partner. Margulies believes that the first step towards the complex cell was a merger between a swimming bacterium and a fermenting bacterium. This is the ancestral symbiotic cell, and makes up most of the modern cell. Next was a respiring bacterium, *paracoccus*.[52]

---

[52]Lynn Margulies, *The Symbiotic Planet, op. cit.*

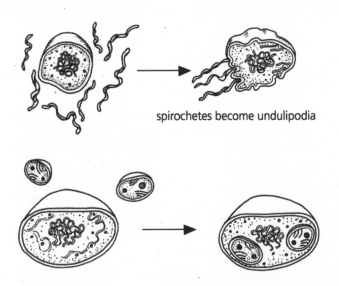

spirochetes become undulipodia

cyanobacterium and aerobic bacterium
combine in symbyotic relationship

In the midst of the oxygen crisis, this symbiotic arrangement, with oxygen-using bacteria inside, proved very attractive to some. It was the safe place to be in the new, oxygen-rich world. Symbiotic colonies of bacteria began to evolve which could use oxygen and which combined the strengths of their various members. In a modern eurkaryotic cell, the oxygen-using part is an organelle called a mitochondria. Mitochondria today retain many of the characteristics of free-living bacteria. Their internal structure and chemistry is very similar to that of some bacteria.

Other cell structures are like this too. Plant cells contain choloroplasts, the sites of photosynthesis. They also have their own DNA, reproduce independently, and are nearly identical to a bacterium called *prochloron*.

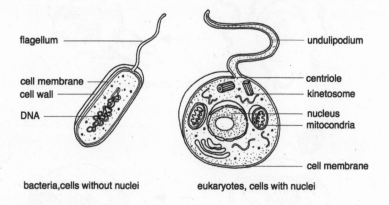

flagellum — undulipodium

cell membrane — centriole
cell wall — kinetosome

DNA — nucleus
— mitocondria

— cell membrane

bacteria,cells without nuclei   eukaryotes, cells with nuclei

Procaryotic and eucaryotic cells compared[53]

The evolution of the eukaryotic cell starts as a colony of bacteria, living a symbiotic life for mutual benefit. Over time, the internal structure changed, with much of the genetic material coming together into a central nucleus. The process by which the DNA in the nucleus of a eukaryotic cell divides is much more complex than in a bacterium. The details of this division are aided by structures that also might have had bacterial origins.

The new large nucleus now contained most of the cell's genes. That is, it contained most of the templates needed to build the molecules from which the parts of the cell were made. Again, this provided a description of the cell that was the key to the maintenance of its wholeness.

This is the story of perhaps the greatest step in life's evolution. It is certainly clear that those new organisms that exploited oxygen survived much better than those that could not. The descendants of the latter now remain mostly in specialised environments, including our guts. But symbiosis was the key to the emergence of a new level of the organisation of life.

These new, more complex cells had some striking advantages over bacteria. Some were much more mobile. They contained undulating hair-like protrusions to propel them along. These are likely to have evolved from

---

[53] *ibid.* p. 45.

spirochaetes, whip-like bacteria with similar properties. This mobility and their larger size helped in gathering food. Their extra complexity enabled them to cope with a wider range of conditions.

These new creatures flourished. For about two billion years, until the animals, plants and fungi developed, they and the bacteria were the only forms of life. Those creatures that have cells with nuclei but are not animals, plants or fungi are called protists.

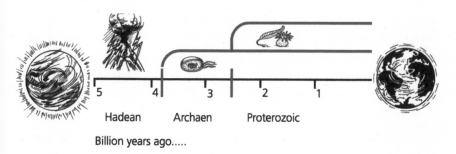

Hadean   Archaen   Proterozoic

Billion years ago.....

The Proterozoic age followed the Archean age. Both bacteria and protists flourished

Many of the protists are single-celled creatures, like amoeba and paramecium. But some are also multi-cellular, like slime molds, seaweeds, kelp and sponges. (In fact there are multi-cellular forms of bacteria too.) These multi-cellular forms generally develop as clones of a single cell. There is very little specialisation of cells, unlike the plants and animals that were still to come.

> **You** And isn't a multi-cellular creature also a form of collaboration rather than competition?

> **Me** Exactly.

Multi-cellular forms, too, had many advantages, with their size contributing to the stability of their local environment. For a cell that is part of a multi-cellular form, much of importance in its local environment consists of its sibling cells. By enhancing the survival of its local environment, the cell enhances its own survival. It is an example of life co-evolving with its environment so that the life form and local environment become closely matched.

COMPLEX CREATURES: THE PHANEROZOIC AGE

The story moves on to the final part, the last 570 million years out of 5 billion, when most of the standard evolutionary story took place. It is the story of life as told mainly by the fossil record. Most of the earlier parts have been discovered only within the last few decades. Earlier life left no fossils, and its discovery awaited the development of more subtle techniques.

As the Proterozoic age drew to its close, oxygen began to build up towards modern levels. High in the stratosphere, ultraviolet radiation turned some of that oxygen into ozone. (Oxygen molecules normally consist of two oxygen atoms; ozone molecules are made up of three oxygen atoms.) This layer of ozone then absorbed most of the ultraviolet, creating a shield that protected life, and made possible its spread onto land.

As oxygen built up, carbon dioxide levels fell still further. The Earth cooled; another ice age followed. A major change in the geological record marks this point. After it, life proliferated as never before, now onto land as well as in the seas. Creatures with hard body parts evolved and so fossils began to appear. This is the Phanerozoic age.

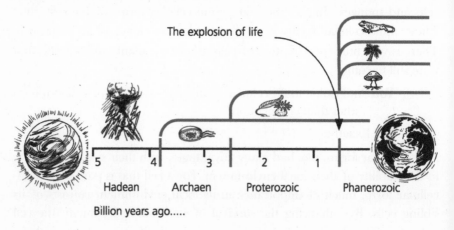

The explosion of life

Hadean   Archaen   Proterozoic   Phanerozoic

Billion years ago.....

Biologists now divide life into six kingdoms: bacteria, archaea, protists, fungi, plants and animals.

By the beginning of the Phanerozoic, the first three of these were well established. In the Phanerozoic, multi-cellular forms of protists evolved into the fungi, plants and animals. All of them (and that includes all of us) are really symbiotic colonies of cells, which in turn are symbiotic colonies of bacteria. The three new kingdoms each developed as expressions of a new and specialised life strategy.

The fungi specialise in external digestion. They give off chemicals that transform some of what is around them into the chemicals they need as food, which they then absorb. They often live in a symbiotic relationship with plants, supplying the nitrogen and phosphorus the plants need. Plants use sunlight as an energy source to enable them to build themselves, mostly out of carbon dioxide and water. They give off oxygen as a by-product. Animals take in oxygen and use it in a controlled combustion process as an energy source, with carbon dioxide as a by-product. Animals generally need fairly complex chemicals (carbohydrates, proteins and fats) as the starting points for forming and re-forming themselves. To get these chemicals, they eat plants, animals or animal waste products. Their waste products and dead bodies also feed the plants, fungi, bacteria and protists.

The parts go round and round. Oxygen and carbon dioxide are cycled between plants and animals. Some creatures build up bigger bodies from simpler parts. Some creatures turn the bodies of other creatures back into their simpler parts. Bacteria, archaea, protists, fungi, plants and animals are all intricately enmeshed in this. It is a grand whirlpool pattern made up of smaller whirlpool patterns made up of still smaller whirlpool patterns.

Recycling is the essence of the pattern of life. It started at a local level with the bacteria. The possibilities expanded with new forms of bacteria and then protists. With the development of fungi, plants and animals, many new pathways opened along which the parts could be recycled. As a result, the total mass of life on Earth expanded tremendously – the explosion of life.

Early in their evolution, plants developed a form of sexual reproduction more familiar to us. Some of their cells divided in half without first doubling the genes within them, so that each of the new cells had only half the complement of genes. These then combined with similar cells from another individual. The result was a cell with the full amount of genetic material, half from one parent and half from the other.

This sexual reproduction from specialised cells was part of a general pattern, where plants came to be made up of parts whose cells were specialised for different functions – roots, stems, seeds, leaves and ultimately flowers. Each individual now was a symbiotic colony of parts, each of which supported the others in its own way. This specialisation allowed greater variety in life strategies: leaves could catch the light while roots absorbed water from under the ground.

MAINTAINING WHOLENESS

The first cells, the bacteria, had a wholeness that was more than a whirlpool-like unity because they had genetic material that acted as templates for the molecules of which they were made. In the more complex eukaryotic cells, the templates, the genetic material, are mostly concentrated in the nucleus. Again, they provide the description that maintains the wholeness of the eukaryotic cell.

Multi-celled creatures with specialised cells involve another level of description. The specialised cells within one creature can be very different. In plants, the difference between pollen, petal, leaf, bark, and root is striking. Yet it is as nothing compared to the difference between cells in animals: white blood cells are similar to amoeba while bone cells are more like a tree trunk. Nerve cells, skin cells, muscle cells, light sensitive cells in the eye – all are so different that in isolation they might be thought totally unrelated.

All the cells in a multi-cellular creature contain identical genetic material, but only some is used in each type of cell. Only the templates for the parts needed for that cell are active. It is as though the genes for many different creatures were combined in one place, but with only some of them switched on at any one time. The next level of description of a multi-cellular creature is that which determines which genes are switched on and off in a particular cell. The switching on and off of genes is an essential

94

part of the functioning of an organism, beyond just the growth and specialisation of the cells. Switching on a gene means that the chemical for which it is a template gets produced. It is largely under the control of hormones, which are a set of chemicals which circulate through an organism, as a general control system.

At any of these levels of wholeness – bacteria, eukaryotic cell, or multi-cellular organism – co-ordination at an overall level replaces any competition between the parts. Where it fails you get disease, as cancer is growth out of control of the whole.

The earliest plants were the mosses and liverworts. Ferns with seeds followed them. These were the first land plants. They formed the first forests between 345 and 225 million years ago. Our modern coal fields are the remains of some of those early forests, showing that the recycling was not complete. By burning that coal today we are returning carbon dioxide to the atmosphere which was removed from it by those forests when they were alive.

The first conifers appeared about 225 million years ago. They relied on the weather to distribute their seeds. The first flowering plants appeared about 123 million years ago. They evolved together with the insects in a symbiosis in which flowers attract the insects to the nectar within, and in the process of travelling from plant to plant, the insects pollinate the plants.

Animals, like plants, are complex symbiotic colonies of specialised cells. The distinction that is now made between animal-like, multi-celled protists and what are now considered true animals was that the latter developed from an embryo. Another key feature of true animals is sophisticated communication between cells, particularly through a nervous system. The combination of nerve cells and muscle cells allowed synchronised contraction of the muscle cells to produce co-ordinated movement. The combination of nerve cells and cells that responded to light or to chemicals in the water or air gave sight, smell and taste.

These organisms provide useful metaphors for the kinds of co-operative societies dealt with later. They have a variety of parts, each working together in their own way for the better survival of the whole, with competition between the parts suppressed. Their common wholeness is described in the templates – the genetic material that is the same in each cell but expressed differently in different cells. They have a communication system to help them identify problems and solve them in a co-ordinated manner.

The earliest animals were some primitive worms, dating from about 700 million years ago, actually before the start of the Phanerozoic age. From these came the segmented worms, then the other segmented creatures, like those with external skeletons (trilobites, crabs, shrimp, insects and spiders). From some of the segmented worms developed creatures with a chord of nerves running through their length. When this became encased in bone it formed the first spinal chord, and from this came the fish (513 million years ago), then the amphibians (345 million years), the reptiles (245 million years) and finally the mammals and the birds (210 million years). Over time the mixture of creatures changed. The parts were rearranged in different ways. New pathways along which the parts were cycled arose while old ones disappeared.

CATASTROPHE AND DIVERSITY

The changes in the mixture of life forms was not usually smooth. The pattern of the Archean and Proterozoic ages – crises followed by the emergence of new forms – appears to be the normal pattern. The Phanerozoic, too, is marked by massive crises, sudden great extinctions when a large proportion of the life forms vanished, followed by the development of new forms.

About 250 million years ago there was a massive extinction which killed off 90% of all species of life.[54] Although the causes aren't too clear, it seems that there was a slow decline in species for a few million years before it, and then a sudden catastrophic event. There was slow climatic change caused by the coming together of some of the continents. This also resulted in a

---

[54] Peter D. Ward, *Rivers in Time, The search for clues to Earth's mass extinctions,* Columbia University Press, New York, 2000, is the source for this and the following discussion.

period of huge volcanic activity that released vast amounts of carbon dioxide. The carbon dioxide in the seas was a direct killer, but it also led to a sudden temperature rise of 5–10°C. That was the catastrophe which did most of the killing.

You Shades of today's fears of global warming.

Me Exactly. That extreme extinction event was the result of runaway global warming and is the potential worst outcome of what we are now doing.

This catastrophe marks the start of the Triassic period in the geological record. It took millions of years to re-stock the land and the seas. Even the 10% of species that survived were severely depleted. The few survivors found themselves in a wide-open world with very little competition, so they flourished and diversified into the new niches. This was a good time for reptiles, and the first dinosaurs appeared. The first true mammals also appeared at this time, but mostly they were small insectivores and tree dwellers.

There was another mass extinction at the end of the Triassic, 200 million years ago. Although not as severe as the one which started it, it is still one of the big five extinctions. Again, it seems that a series of environmental problems, like big volcanic eruptions, led up to it. This time the final catastrophe seems to have been triggered by a four or five-mile-wide meteor colliding with the Earth, forming the 70-mile-wide Manicouagan Crater in Quebec.

This extinction event marks the end of the Triassic and the start of the Jurassic period. The aftermath was that the dinosaurs became the dominant land animals. It took the two major mass extinctions for this to come about. They weathered the extinction with only modest losses and were dominant for about 120 million years until the mass extinction event 65 million years ago.

The final cause of that extinction was a now notorious meteor or comet. It was at least six miles in diameter and hit the Earth in the sea near Yucatan, Mexico, creating a 180-mile-wide crater and massive tidal waves. More than half the Earth's vegetation burned in the weeks after the impact. Acid rain made the seas too acid for much life, and global warming resulted from the release of carbon dioxide. Even before this time, though, many species were already in decline or were going extinct. It seems that there were three separate causes: climate change from carbon dioxide emissions, sea level change and then the meteor.

The mass extinction event 65 million years ago killed off most of the dinosaurs, leaving the birds as their only descendants. A few mammals also survived and went on to become the dominant form of life. They went through a burst of evolution, starting with many very small mammals. Then, about 40 million years ago, the Earth cooled, leading to the spread of grasslands that favoured the evolution of large mammals. There were many giant mammals: many elephant species, mammoths and mastodons, giant camels and enormous ground sloths, giant dogs, cats and bears too. By about six million years ago, the world appeared nearly in the form that it was in when humanity evolved.

The final chapter in the story of life starts about 2.5 million years ago. Again, a variety of events led to more cooling, and the Earth entered a period of ice ages. Since then the climate has oscillated between longer ice ages and briefer interglacial periods. This cooling brought about a pulse of extinctions. The modern extinction started then. Again, it started with climate change a few million years before the major event that provided the *coup de grâce*. Thirty per cent of North American land mammals went extinct at the onset of the ice age. However, the knockout punch for the larger mammals was delivered about 11,000 years ago, when two-thirds of North and South America's larger mammals suddenly disappeared over a period of about 1,000 years. This coincided with the arrival of humans in the Americas. It was the first chapter in the story of humanity as a global cancer.

> **You** Doesn't all this talk of extinctions and survivors mean that at a time of crisis the fittest survive? And you keep writing about symbiosis, but you barely mention competition and survival of the fittest. Surely you aren't just going to ignore them?

Me I think I've spelled out enough of the history so that I can tackle this issue of competition and fitness directly now. Just for starters, I'll answer your first question. At a time of crisis the meaning of fitness changes, so different creatures survive than survived before it.

SYMBIOSIS AND COMPETITION

By now the intricate interconnectedness of life is very clear. All creatures rely on many others to provide their food and shelter, decompose the accumulated rubbish all create, and generally provide the rest of all the cycles of which they are part. The environment for each is all of the rest. The life cycle of any creature cannot be understood without understanding its environment. All creatures are simultaneously separate individuals and parts of a larger whole.

From this perspective, fitness means fitting in the sense that a piece in a jigsaw puzzle fits into the hole left for it. That hole is the particular way of life, the niche, of that individual. Fitness certainly does not mean a general superiority of one creature over another. A niche can also be seen as an opportunity, a possible way of living for something. An organism evolves and finds its place in its conversation with its environment. The niche is the other side of that conversation.

Under normal conditions, when there is no crisis in progress, virtually all the niches available get filled. In natural grassland there will be a mixture of grazing animals, each with somewhat different teeth and digestive systems so they can eat different mixtures of the vegetation. There will be different birds, each with differently shaped beaks specialised to eating different sizes of insects, or those that live at different depths under the surface. There will be some animals specialised to feed on virtually every one of the plants and some predators and parasites that eat virtually all of the animals.

Of course, the jigsaw puzzle analogy is somewhat limited. The edges of the biological holes are not sharp as in the puzzle. There is a certain amount of overlap between the niches of one creature and another. It is in these areas of overlap that competition comes into play. It provides a jostling for position that clarifies this overlap and leaves the niches more distinct.

> **You** You are giving competition a very marginal role then?
>
> **Me** Well it's a very important role. The interconnections and symbiosis determine the overall shape of the pattern, the mixture of creatures and how they live. The clarity with which the parts of this pattern fit together; the closeness of the fit, comes from competition. That is what I understand by survival of the fittest.

Another limitation of the jigsaw puzzle analogy is that the shapes are fixed, while biological niches are continually changing. With no environmental crisis, the changes are small and slow. Creatures become highly specialised, very closely adapted to the conditions around them, their food species, symbiotic species, predators and so on. Then along comes a crisis: the primordial soup runs out, oxygen begins to appear, an ice age begins or ends, a mass extinction event occurs or maybe it is something much smaller and more local. Then the shape of all the holes changes. The niches are no longer what they were. The intricate web of support is rendered. It is no good being a mighty dinosaur, capable of killing any large animal around, and especially those puny little mammals. If the food of your food goes, you go too. In a crisis, the fitness of an individual animal or species is not relevant. It is the set of relationships in the whole ecosystem around it that counts.

After a crisis there is no longer as close a matching of life forms. New pathways become available. New strategies for living can emerge. A crisis favours generalists, creatures which can feed off a wide range of others or who can live in varied conditions. There is a rapid development of new forms of life.

> **You** Perhaps there is a lesson in there for us. If the global cancer triggers a major crisis, then generalist groups and individuals will have an advantage.
>
> **Me** Yes, I agree.

Under the new conditions, some creatures find they have some very useful abilities, perhaps developed for another purpose. Fish living in shallow shore waters who learned to breathe air a little and use their fins to push along the bottom might find they could survive on land a little. They are already adapted to the new conditions. At first the new forms don't have to be very well adapted to the conditions. The first land animals couldn't walk very well. The first birds couldn't fly very well. Competitive pressures soon sort out a new set of niches with specialised, well-adapted creatures. As walking or flying predators appeared, their prey learned to run and fly fast. As the new set of niches becomes filled, change slows down and a normal period arrives.

> **You** I think I'm beginning to get the idea. You aren't saying that competition isn't important, just that this symbiosis business and being part of the web of life is actually the major part of what counts.

> **Me** Yes, that's right. The image of nature as a war is a projection onto nature of a market economic system! It is very recent, only appearing since Darwin in the last century. It replaced a projection of feudalism onto nature, 'God's harmony' with everything in its hierarchical place.

> **You** Aren't you trying to create a projection onto nature of your view of society? What is nature really like?

> **Me** I suppose that is what I am doing (although it's not just my view). What is nature really like? I suppose a sage would say that nature 'just is'.

> **You** I'm not completely satisfied yet. Can we go back to competition? What about the competition between male animals for dominance or access to females? Surely that is a major part of their life?

> **Me** OK. Within one species the same principles apply, and we can sometimes even begin to glimpse another level of organisation.

Within one species the overlap between niches is especially strong. All the foxes in a wood eat the same prey. All the rabbits like the same plants. What generally happens is that the niches for creatures of the same species are geographic. Individuals or groups have their own territories within which there is sufficient to meet their needs. Competition again appears at the boundaries of the territories. Birds sing in large part to say "this is my territory."

For many animals, other members of their own species are of major importance in their environment. At the very least, they need them to mate. Thus it is not surprising that when competition arises between members of a species, it is usually minimised. Often there is a ritual or rule that determines which creature wins. With certain butterflies, the first one on a particular leaf has priority. With many animals threatening postures are enough to see off a rival.

The issue between two rival animals is to see which one gets to mate, or gets the territory. This is a matter of communication between creatures with very limited means of communication. If the appropriate criterion is the size and showiness of your tail feathers, then a display will settle the issue. If it is a matter of strength, then a fight is needed. However, animal fights rarely end in death or serious injury. They generally end when it is clear who will win.

It is striking how many different animals live in groups: flocks, herds, schools, prides, or whatever. For these animals, the benefits of being in a group clearly outweigh competitive pressures from sharing a niche. Being part of a group can give protection from predators (grazing animals), help with care of offspring (lions), co-operation in hunting (dogs). Some of the social insects have very specialised forms. An individual ant or termite is barely a separate creature. It may be able to gather food, or produce eggs or defend the colony, but not any of the other tasks. It is more like a cell in the super-organism that is the colony.

Imagine you are watching a large flock of starlings, hundreds or even thousands of birds.[55] You notice a main group and various smaller groups, constantly changing. A few birds circle high in the air watching for

[55] See for example, <u>A murmuration of starlings</u>: video from YouTube

predators. One or two take off to the next field to search for food. A few more peel off from the main group to join them. If they are successful and settle onto that field, others will see them and join them and soon the bulk of the flock will leave its present location and join them. If the watchers signal danger (you perhaps), the whole lot will suddenly take off and fly away.

Birds are the ultimate symbol of freedom. None of those starlings tells any of the others what to do. They live in a flock, choosing their roles from moment to moment in support of the flock, synchronising their behaviour with each other, because that is what it is to be a starling. Freedom and collaboration are in no sense in conflict with one another.

How's that for a metaphor for a collaborative society?

8 The co-operative ape: the early human story

The last chapter set a biological context for humanity. Now it is time to look at what it means to be human. The last chapter dispelled the myth that the natural world is inherently competitive and warlike. This one does the same for humanity.

Today it is very common for people to find themselves in situations where the appropriate response seems competitive or warlike rather than co-operative. People have become very skilled at being competitive. Our most sophisticated technology is that of war. Human history suggests that this has been the case only since the advent of what we call civilisation – very recent in our evolutionary story. This chapter will trace this aspect of humanity's history. The story is of an animal whose niche, whose speciality, was working in co-operation within small social bands, sharing food which had been gathered and hunted, sharing child care, learning from their ancestors' experience, etc. Our big brains, languages and cultures evolved to make this possible. Our physiology and personalities evolved as animals who were co-ordinating their group actions well beyond that of any other mammals.

ORIGINS

In the family tree of life, humans are on the mammalian branch, which appeared some 210 million years ago. We are part of the primate sub-branch, which includes monkeys, apes and others like lemurs, tarsiers and lorises. The first primates appeared about 70 million years ago. About 20 million years ago, out of Africa came the Oak Ape, *Dryopithecus*, the ancestor of all the modern apes, including the chimpanzees, gorillas, orang-utans and humans.

You Don't you mean the apes and the humans?

Me No, I think it is pure conceit to give us a group by ourselves. We are all considered part of the biological family *hominidae*.[56]

Our closest relatives here are the chimpanzees, which is probably why they are so appealing to us. In fact, our genetic makeup differs from that of the chimps by only 1%. It is an important 1%, but it is nonetheless clear that in terms of our physical makeup we are just a variation on the ape theme. Chimps are highly intelligent animals. They can do simple counting and fractions, and can recognise simple geometrical shapes. Someone has estimated that chimps have an IQ (in human terms) of 80[57], which is not bad at all.

There have been many experiments in which people have tried to teach chimps human language, with a certain amount of success. Chimps do not have the muscular control of their faces and vocal cords needed to produce words, but they can learn to use sign language, or to communicate using special keyboards and they can understand limited human speech. They tend to combine words with gestures. The Bonobo chimps seem to have the most advanced abilities. They can understand sentences of the complexity of:

"Get a Coke and give it to Rose. The Coke is on the table there."

"Get the ball that's outdoors." (another one was in view)

Their language ability is limited to objects and events in their direct experience, and is comparable to that of a child of two or so.

Chimps are very social animals with active and intricate social lives. They live in bands for mutual protection and companionship, spending much time grooming each other. They can spontaneously learn to use objects around them as simple tools. They use twigs to fish ants from holes in wood. Groups of chimps hunt monkeys: some will chase the monkey into an ambush formed by several others. Fighting is common among chimps, but their social bonds are so important to them that fights usually end in

---

[56] Desmond Morris, in his classic book, *The Naked Ape*, made this point very well.

[57] From Helen Fisher, *The Sex Contract, The Evolution of Human Behaviour*, Granada, 1982.

reconciliation.. "Within a minute of a fight having ended the two former opponents may rush towards each other, kiss and embrace long and fervently and then proceed to groom each other."[58]

There is a dominance hierarchy of males and females in a chimp band. The most dominant male has the greatest sexual access to the females when they are in heat. His function is to protect them from attack or annoyance, especially by other males. To maintain his dominance he needs the active assistance of the females. In *Chimpanzee Politics*, Frans de Waal describes the intricate manoeuvres chimps get up to as one male, or perhaps a pair, will challenge another for dominance. "Whole passages of Machiavelli seem to be directly applicable to chimpanzee behaviour".[59] Deception is part of their normal repertoire of behaviour. This is significant in what it tells us about chimpanzee mental abilities: for a chimp to be able to deceive another, it must be able to imagine what it is like to be that other chimp.

---

[58] Frans de Waal, *Chimpanzee Politics*, Jonathon Cape, 1982., p. 41.

[59] *op. cit.* p. 19.

Chimps have friendships, but do not form permanent sexual bonds. Female chimps do not normally mate except when they are in heat. When a female chimp is in heat, the other males pay special attention to her, and may bring her gifts of food. Otherwise, food is not generally given by one chimp to another, although a group will share eating an animal they have killed.

Humans and chimps parted company around four million years ago. The climate had changed somewhat; the forests were shrinking, but there were opportunities for apes to exploit on the edges of the forest. Perhaps it helped if you could run out of the forest into a nearby clump of vegetation, grab some fruit or nuts and carry them back to the safety of the forest. To do this you had to use your hands and walk on your feet only. (Apes can walk on their legs and carry things with their hands if they want to, but normally they walk on all fours, putting some of their weight on their knuckles. Like most mammals, their backs are suited to supporting their body's weight at both ends.)

The apes that exploited this new way of living soon became adapted to it. The angle of their hips changed, their feet changed, the angle of their heads changed. Their backs – bone and muscle – adapted to standing on one end to support the entire weight of their bodies. These upright apes, *Australopithecus*, were our earliest direct ancestors. Other than their upright stance, they were like other apes. Their brain size was the same, and we can presume that they were as intelligent and social as the other apes.

There is another way in which humans differ from the other apes, one mentioned less often than our big brains and upright stance. We are by far the sexiest of the apes. Our women are sexually receptive even when they cannot conceive; they have lost the ape's distinguishing physical signs of being on heat. Women have sex when they are pregnant, during menstruation, and on into old age beyond the childbearing years. This increased sexuality probably dates from very early in human evolution, at the time of *Australopithecus*. For us, sex has taken on an additional function.

It is not just to conceive children: it also promotes bonding between people, a first step towards increased sociability and culture[60].

Standing upright might have had its advantages for food gathering, but it also created certain problems. The change in the angle of the pelvis disrupted the easy passage of the infant through the birth canal. The difficulty humans have in giving birth started at this early point, and was compounded much later when human brain sizes increased. The solution was that babies were born slightly earlier, and thus smaller, than other ape babies. These less mature babies needed more care than earlier ape babies, so the friendly attention of the men was very welcome. The food sharing which was offered to a sexually receptive female previously would be of great benefit to a sexually receptive female with an infant. Any increased care and attention would promote the survival of mother and child. Thus was born what Helen Fisher calls 'the sex contract', a close tie between two people for mutual support based on sexual attraction, but not just to produce babies. It developed into our present sexiness and contributed to what we call falling in love.

Standing upright itself, with the new angle of the pelvis, might have promoted increased sexuality as the sexual organs were displayed more directly. Eye contact was enhanced and face-to-face sex, with its greater intimacy, became more favoured. Various physical differences between humans and the other apes are likely to have arisen at this time and would have increased human sexiness – loss of most body hair, skin that is more sensitive to touch, enlarged breasts (as a reminder of the sensuality of nursing?), larger penises, and prolonged sex. (For chimps it lasts just 15 seconds.)

From this early stage, becoming more like what we would call human was to do with increased sociability. The early bonds between men and women were a step towards human culture: one could even speculate that face-to-face sex, close eye contact and more kissing meant that the muscles of the face and mouth became more flexible, allowing subtler movements. As the

---

[60] There is a very good discussion of this in Helen Fisher's *The Sex Contract, op. cit.*

couple had more to do with each other, communication between them would become much more important.

> **You** So it was the *Australopithecus* women who first started saying to their men, "We need to communicate more!"

> **Me** Probably yes! My speculation is that the physical changes for increased sexiness pre-adapted people for better communication and speech.

Mary Leakey discovered a famous set of fossilised footprints of a small group of *Australopithicus* in Tanzania. As Helen Fisher interprets it:

> "The time was the beginning of the wet season some 3.6 million years ago... On this afternoon a large adult hominid, about four feet eight inches tall, was strolling through the damp volcanic ash. Beside him was his companion, a smaller (probably female) hominid about four feet tall. They strode through the muck together, almost rubbing shoulders. Behind the larger individual, another smaller one followed, carefully stepping in the footsteps of the leader. ...Mary Leakey thinks that the two adults who walked side by side almost four million years ago were holding hands; that all three were playing."[61]

So now we have an upright ape, with hands free to carry, manipulate, and use tools, and with an increased sexuality to promote bonds between individuals. These bonds created collaborations that would have been to the benefit of the individuals and the whole band: more efficient gathering of food, protection and child care.

With this heightened sexuality, no longer linked only to procreation, and with the advantages that sexual bonds brought, sexual bonds may have developed between two men or two women. These, too, would have been beneficial to survival. Two men might become a more efficient hunting team. Two women might share the care of children conceived with their male lovers. As no offspring are produced, homosexual bonds would have been relatively infrequent, as they are now. Nonetheless, it is consistent with

[61] Helen Fisher, *op cit.* p. 79.

this pattern to see homosexuality appearing very early. It seems to be a small part of the normal human sexual repertoire, just as red hair is a small part of the normal variation of human hair colourings.

TOWARDS MODERN HUMANS

Australopithecus may have been an upright-walking, sexy, social ape, but was still a long way from the big-brained, talking, cultured people of today. The next major change occurred about 1.6 million years ago, probably triggered again by climate change. The Earth entered another phase of ice ages which continues today, so far as we know. Because these ice ages are so much more recent than the ice ages 2.5 billion and 570 million years ago, there is much more evidence.

A few million years ago, a new type of plant evolved which could live more efficiently on lower levels of carbon dioxide, and carbon dioxide levels fell still lower. Various other conditions were significant too: the continents had shifted to suitable positions, with Antarctica over the South Pole where it could support an ice cap, and a ring of land around the North Pole on which an ice cap could form. The result was that the climate became unstable and could easily be triggered into or out of an ice age about 1.6 million years ago. Since then the Earth has oscillated into and out of ice ages regularly – triggered partly by wobbles in the Earth's orbit.

The next stage on from *Australopithecus* – with much larger brains – started to appear at the beginning of this ice age period, 1.6 million years ago. But it wasn't until the beginning of the last interglacial, 130,000 years ago, that fully modern people appeared with bodies more or less the same as ours. So most of the time since big-brained humans appeared, the Earth has been in an ice age.

The dramatically changing climate of the past 1.6 million years created crisis after crisis to which all life on Earth, including developing humanity, had to adapt. During the inter-glacial periods, huge parts of the land were covered in forest – temperate in cooler areas and rainforest in the tropics. During the ice ages, ice sheets covered large parts of Europe, Asia and North America. Below this was largely tundra. The rainforests shrank and fragmented into small, separate areas. When the next inter-glacial arrived the forests and rainforests rapidly re-grew and joined. This repeated fragmentation and re-joining is probably responsible for the enormous variety of species found in rainforests, which are now fragmented by us. Crisis after crisis also favoured the evolution of more generalist animals, like humans.

Like chimpanzees and gorillas, *Australopithecus* had a brain size of about 450cc. The earliest of our bigger brained ancestors, *Homo habilis*, had a brain twice that size (and we have brains about three times that size.). Their hands were almost as dextrous as ours. With their remains have been found simple stone tools, probably used for crushing nuts, breaking open bones to expose the marrow, other food preparation, scraping, cutting and hammering. They did only a little shaping of the natural stone, choosing stones with a useful shape to start with.

Later, and somewhat bigger-brained, *Homo erectus* first appeared in Africa about 1.6 million years ago. By 730,000 years ago their descendants had spread to the Middle East and southern Europe. By 250,000 years ago they had spread throughout Europe and Asia.

They used quite a variety of stone tools, carefully shaped. They made hand axes, choppers, chisels, scrapers, cleavers, awls, anvils and hammerstones. To do this they had developed quite elaborate techniques for breaking and shaping stones. They also built dwellings and used fire. With this level of sophistication, they were likely to have used animal bladders to carry water and use animal skins for clothing in the cold ice age winters.

This is a long way from the lifestyle of the Oak Ape, ancestor to all the apes. This is culture: people learning detailed ways of doing things from each other. It wasn't only the bodies (including brains) of our ancestors that were evolving, their ideas were evolving too. The technologies of making tools and the lifestyles associated with them were passed from person to person and from generation to generation. For these early humans the intricate web of life in which all creatures are enmeshed now included their ancestors. Human culture – relationships with other humans – came to be more and more important as part of the environment of an individual human.

The evolution of bigger brains and early human cultures were two aspects of the same process. Bigger brains allowed the understanding needed for the developing culture, which in turn created the pressure for the elaboration of the brain.

Part of this process must have been the development of language. Early language would have been very close to direct experience and memory, a few steps beyond what a chimpanzee can learn today. It was a language of objects, and manipulating objects, simple stories of how to do this, and what happens when you do that. What can you eat and how do you prepare it? Where and when are these plants found? How do you catch and kill these animals? This made a major difference in the life experience of early people. Along with their direct experiences of food, other creatures and the weather, they had experiences shaped by language. There were associations between certain stones and the tools they could make, names that linked whole classes of objects. Thinking, as we know it, was born.

MODERN HUMANS

Homo sapiens seems to have evolved in Africa too, descended from *Homo erectus* populations there. They first appeared around 130,000 years ago, and they too spread widely. They had arrived in the Middle East about 90,000 years ago, had spread throughout Europe and even reached Australia by 40,000 years ago, but did not get to Japan or Siberia until about 30,000 years ago. They reached North America some 10-15,000 years ago. In the middle of the last ice age, with so much water locked up in the ice sheets, the sea level was much lower. There were land bridges between Siberia and Alaska, and only a short distance by sea to Australia.

By about 60,000-40,000 years ago, in the middle of the last ice age, came fully modern humans, *Homo sapiens sapiens*. At around this time a new level of culture appears in human remains. This was the time of cave paintings of animals and people, which appear beautiful even by modern artistic standards. Tools with great aesthetic appeal appear. This was a time of ritual burial – bodies carefully laid out with a variety of objects. Beautiful carved statues have been found, in the form of abstractions of a pregnant woman. These are generally interpreted as symbols of a fertility goddess. Abstract thought, symbolism and religion had arrived. This is quite recent on the time scale of human evolution. There appears to have been very little further development of human bodies and brains since. If an infant from that time were raised in a modern western city, it would probably be indistinguishable from the rest of its new family. Its speech would be fully fluent and with a modern accent. It might grow up to be a nuclear physicist or a politician.

You More likely unemployed. You say a politician, but didn't you also say that chimpanzees were good politicians?

Me I said that chimpanzees' social manipulations were Machiavellian, but they are not capable of giving a speech showing that their actions are for the public good!

The point is that the level of complexity of human culture that had evolved by the time *Homo sapiens sapiens* appeared was fully modern. Brains capable of handling the level of abstraction their cultures required are also capable of handling the abstractions of modern science. Languages subtle enough for their purposes were subtle enough for the careful shadings of truth of modern politicians. What continued to evolve were the ideas, technologies and forms of social organisation.

The early *Homo sapiens sapiens* lived in small bands, of perhaps 30 to 50 people. They were wandering gatherers and hunters. This has been the principal way of life of humans from the very beginning. It began to be displaced with the beginnings of agriculture about 10,000 years ago, and then still more with the advent of cities and large scale social organisation, about 5,000 years ago. Substantial populations lived in this way as late as the 19th century, but only small isolated pockets of these cultures are left today.

The gathering/hunting way of life required a very detailed and sophisticated understanding of the life cycles of plants and animals. Which parts are good to eat? Which have medicinal properties or can be used as poisons to hunt others? How do you make tools for carrying, hunting or shelter out of stone, bone, wood, or animal parts? Where are the game animals or the ripe edible plants this week?

All of this was wrapped in a rich social life in which people collaborated in finding and preparing food, and caring for their children and their old people. Talk around the campfires might be of the availability of food, but also gossip about the doings and mis-doings of the people in their own and neighbouring bands. Our complex brains and languages evolved with and were formed by the need to cope with this rich knowledge of the natural and social environment. Most adults knew most of what was needed to thrive. By contrast, in modern cultures the cumulative and stored knowledge is much greater, but any individual knows very little of that total.

A major function of culture has always been the maintenance of the bonds between people, because interactions with other people make up a very large part of the environment in which people live. Many cultural devices evolved to support this: rituals, music, dance and ceremonies.

> **You** Let me get this clear: are you saying that the purpose of music and dance is to maintain bonds between people?

> **Me** Yes, I imagine that they evolved fairly soon after abstract thought evolved, and for exactly that reason. Any aspect of developing culture that supported group coherence would aid group survival and would be likely to continue. That is also why music and dance have such a strong emotional impact.

The development of abstract thought meant that human minds could add extra layers of association to their experience. Not only could they distinguish tigers but could recognise that many different animals had the same cat-like qualities. They could even associate aspects of cat-like behaviour with aspects of human behaviour. This is metaphor, the mapping of the qualities of one set of experiences onto another. With this ability to use metaphor, many mysterious patterns which people experienced could be explained in terms of familiar social experiences. So the essential nature of the deer might have been given a separate existence, with human-like qualities: a deer-spirit. If there were few deer around to hunt perhaps this deer-spirit had been offended. This is animism, the explanation of natural patterns in terms of spirits or souls.

Early modern humans would have had a very clear intuitive sense of the picture painted in the last chapter – of the inter-connectedness of all living creatures, of the inherently supportive quality of nature, and also of almost constant chaotic and disruptive change. They would have expressed it in the only vocabulary and images they had available: metaphors expressing natural patterns as human-like spirits. They were clear about their part in this interconnectedness, and treated nature with respect.

> "...for hunter-gatherers themselves, a central concern has been their relationship with the creatures they harvest. In this form of management, people trust that if they do the right things, the world will stay as it should; the creatures and plants they eat will feel welcome and know they are respected, and will therefore continue to make themselves available."[62]

This respect generally applied to other people as well, and reflected the nature of gather-hunter social organisation.

> "The egalitarian individualism of hunter-gatherer societies, arguably their greatest achievement and their most compelling lesson for other peoples, relies on many kinds of respect."[63]

This was the time of the goddess cultures. Lovely statues and images of a pregnant woman, somewhat abstracted with no details of face or hands, are found associated with many ancient cultures. They are likely to have symbolised nature, what the ancient Greeks called Gaia, the Earth goddess.

> **You** You seem to be romanticising these cultures. Weren't these also woman-bashing cavemen? Do you really imagine a nature-worshipping, peace-loving, hippy paradise?

> **Me** No, I'm simply trying to counter the view that before civilisations started, humans were ignorant, aggressive savages,

---

[62] Hugh Brody, *The Other Side of Eden, Hunter-gatherers, farmers and the shaping of the world*, Faber and Faber, London, 2001, p. 255.

[63] *ibid*, p. 308.

struggling against the odds for survival. That is why I am emphasising the collaboration, intelligence and intuitive wisdom of early cultures. But I haven't finished with the issue of aggression.

It seems clear that one side of being human is an animal that has taken sociability and collaboration far beyond that of any other animal. We are adapted to it physically, with the language abilities of our brains, faces and vocal chords. With our extended sexuality, and our generalised ability to feel love, we are adapted to it emotionally. Another side of being human is an animal that has taken aggression and conflict far beyond that of any other. These two sides clearly both co-exist in modern cultures. The question is whether the extremes of aggression and conflict exist in all human cultures? Are they – like music, dance, language and our sexiness – a mark of being human or do they only appear under certain conditions?

They do seem to be universal in so-called civilised cultures. And since civilised cultures are a boundary beyond which people rarely look when considering human nature, the myth that they are universal has flourished. To set this straight it is worth considering the range of human cultures that has existed since the appearance of *Homo sopiens sapiens*, some 40-60,000 years ago. From the artifacts left by a prehistoric culture it is very difficult to determining how aggressive the people were. Speculations about this probably say more about the preconceptions of the investigator than of the culture. It is better to consider studies of similar cultures which have existed recently. Some certainly are fierce and warlike, others gentle and peaceful. Here are some examples of the latter.

The people of Tahiti

"The people in general are of the common size of Europeans... their gait easy and genteel and their countenance free, open and lively, never sullied by a sullen or suspicious look — their motions are vigorous, active and graceful and their behaviour to strangers is such as declare at first sight their humane disposition, which is as candid as their countenances seem to indicate, and their courteous, affable and friendly behaviour to each other shows that they have no tincture of barbarity,

116

cruelty, suspicion or revenge. They are ever of an even unruffled temper, so they ought not to be suspected, and an hour's acquaintance is sufficient to repose an entire confidence in them."[64]

"Tahiti in the early 1960's when I began my field work there seemed in regard to gentleness little different than the reports of the late 18th and early 19th century had suggested. ...my own observations during a period of more than two years...indicated in comparison with Western experience and in comparison with reports of many other non-Western societies an extreme lack of angry, hostile, destructive behaviour."[65]

The Yequana of Venezuela

"[There] is a respect for each individual as his own proprietor. ...Deciding what another person should do, no matter what his age, is outside the Yequana vocabulary of behaviours. There is great interest in what everyone does, but no impulse to influence — let alone coerce anyone. A child's will is his motive force. ...The Yequana do not feel that a child's inferior physical strength and dependence upon them imply that they should treat him or her with less respect than an adult. No orders are given a child which run counter to his own inclinations as to how to play, how much to eat, when to sleep, and so on. But where his help is required, he is expected to comply instantly. Commands like 'Bring some water!', 'Chop some wood!', 'Hand me that!', or 'Give the baby a banana!' are given on the same assumption of innate sociality, in the firm knowledge that a child wants to be of service and to join in the work of his people. No one watches to see whether the child obeys — there is no doubt of his will to co-operate. As the social animal he is, he does as he is expected without hesitation and to the very best of his ability."[66]

---

[64] James Morrison, *The Journal of James Morrison*, London, Golden Cockerell Press, 1935, p. 170 (report from 1784).

[65] Robert I. Levy, "Tahitian gentleness and redundant controls", in Montague, Ashley, *Learning Non-aggression*, Oxford University Press, 1978, p. 224.

[66] Jean Liedloff, *The Continuum Concept*, Futura, London, 1975., pp. 78-79.

"One of the most striking differences between the Yequana and any other children I have seen is that they neither fight nor argue among themselves. There is no competitiveness and leadership is established on the initiative of the followers. In the years I spent with them, I never saw a child argue with another, much less fight. The only angry words I did hear were a very rare burst of impatience from an adult with a child who had done something undesirable."[67]

The Buddhist culture of Ladakh[68]

In traditional Ladakh, aggression of any sort is extremely rare: rare enough to say that it is virtually nonexistent. If you ask a Ladakhi to tell you about the last fight he can remember, you are likely to get mischievous answers like 'I'm always beating up my neighbor. Only yesterday I tied him to a tree and cut both his ears off.' Should you get a serious answer, you will be told that there has been no fighting in the village in living memory. Even arguments are rare.

"A concern not to offend or upset one another is deeply rooted in Ladakhi society; people avoid situations that might lead to friction or conflict. When someone transgresses this unwritten law, ...extreme tolerance is the response. And yet concern for community does not have the oppressive effect on the individual that one might have imagined."
"I asked Sonam once, 'Don't you have arguments? We do in the West all the time.'

He thought for a minute. 'Not in the villages, no — well, very very seldom, anyway.'

'How do you manage it?' I asked.

---

[67] *ibid.*, p.95.

[68] Helena Norberg-Hodge, *Ancient Futures, Learning from Ladakh*, Rider, 1991, pp. 46-47. I am including Ladakh because it is such a clear example of the kind of culture I am describing even though it is not an example of a gathering/hunting lifestyle, and as a Buddhist culture, it developed much later than the others.

He laughed. 'What a funny question. We just live with each other, that's all.'

'So what happens if two people disagree — say about the boundaries of their land?'

'They'll talk about it, of course, and discuss it. What would you expect them to do?'

The Fore of New Guinea

"The Fore protoagricultural communities were quite different from anything I had previously encountered. There were no chiefs, priests, medicine men, or the like. Moving about at will and being with whom they like, even the very young enjoyed a striking personal freedom.

Infants rarely cried, and they played confidently with knives, axes and fire. Older children typically enjoyed deferring to the interests and desires of the younger; sibling rivalry was virtually undetectable. A responsive 'sixth sense' seemed to attune the hamlet mates to each other's interests and needs. ...A spontaneous urge to share food, affection, work, trust and pleasure characterised the daily life. Aggression and conflict within communities was unusual and the subject of considerable comment when it occurred."[69]

> **You** That is quite amazing. I find it hard to believe. These descriptions don't sound like people as I know them.
>
> **Me** Yes indeed, it just shows how limited are most people's experience of the possibilities of human nature.

For these cultures, and many others in the anthropological literature, there is a natural, intuitive sociability and co-operation with coercion and aggression rare. The lesson of the starlings applies: they combine freedom and collaborative support. For these people, this is the obvious way people behave.

---

[69]E. Richard Sorenson, "Co-operation and Freedom among the Fore", in Montague, *Learning Non-aggression, op. cit.*, p. 14-15.

You But let me be clear. You are not saying that all cultures were like that before civilisation.

Me No. I've been describing the extreme peaceful end of a spectrum. It simply shows that that extreme is within the bounds of possibility of human nature. I'll take a first look at some of the reasons for the differences now. Unpicking those differences fully is one of the main theme of this book.

Two of the books quoted in this chapter express strong views about why some cultures are more aggressive than others. They point to child-rearing practices as a major factor. Ashley Montague says:

"Years ago Margaret Mead was the first anthropologist to inquire into the origins of aggressiveness in non-literate societies. In her book, *Sex and Temperament in Three Primitive Societies*,[70] she pointed to the existence of a strong association between child-rearing practices and later personality development. The child who received a great deal of attention, whose every need was promptly met, as among the New Guinea Mountain Arapesh, became a gentle, co-operative, unaggressive adult. On the other hand, the child who received perfunctory, intermittent attention, as among the New Guinea Mundugomor, became a selfish, unco-operative, aggressive adult. Later research among nonliterate and civilised peoples has substantially confirmed this relationship, and so do the studies presented in this volume."[71]

Jean Liedloff, in *The Continuum Concept*,[72] and Ashley Montague, in another of his books, *Touching, The Human Significance of the Skin*,[73] are even more specific. Jean Liedloff writes at length about "the in-arms experience", in which an infant in many pre-industrial cultures is continually carried in its mother's arms and is allowed to feed on demand. Ashley Montague describes this same practice as an "external gestation". He says it is

---

[70] Mead, Margaret, *Sex and Temperament in Three Primitive Societies*, Morrow, New York, 1935.

[71] Ashley Montague, *op. cit.* , p. 7.

[72] *op. cit.*

[73] Harper and Row, 1971.

important because human babies are born relatively immature compared to other apes. The sense of security and being cared for in the womb is continued in the early experience of the infant. This provides the foundation for their later views of what the world is like.

> **You** So we are back to permissive parenting. It is not so easy and can result in spoiled children rather than non-aggressive children.
>
> **Me** There is much more to it than that. And 'permissiveness' does not capture the essence of it. The 'child as boss' approach can be as harmful as the 'parent as boss' approach. The key issue is the way the infant learns to see its environment. Is it being supported or is it being opposed?

Both Jean Liedloff and Ashley Montague are clear that child rearing is not the whole story. Ways of caring for infants and children cannot be taken out of the context of the whole culture. There needs to be a consistency between the supportive nature of child-rearing practices and the rest of the culture. This is what Jean Liedloff means by the 'continuum concept'.

THE ORIGINAL AFFLUENT SOCIETY[74]

A quick look at the nature of economic systems in hunter-gatherer societies helps put our own economic system in perspective. Later chapters demonstrate that our system is not the obvious best choice for our future!

There is a common view that life for hunter-gathers was very hard. "Our textbooks compete to convey a sense of impending doom, leaving one to wonder not only how hunters managed to live, but whether, after all, this was living."[75] For the most part, this is projection in order to justify the difficulties of life in civilised cultures. After all, if so many people are poor now, and we have the benefits of agriculture and civilisation, things must have been much worse before that.

---

[74] This is the title of a chapter in the classic book on exchange in hunter-gather societies by Marshall Sahlins, *Stone Age Economics*, Tavistock, 1972.

[75] *ibid.*

The reality was quite different. Early humans were a highly successful species, spreading throughout the world and becoming the top predator wherever they went. If they managed to survive those years when conditions were very difficult, they must have survived quite easily in the normal, good years. This easy life is the view of very many people who have studied modern hunter-gatherer cultures, and inspired Mashall Sahlins to call it "the original affluent society".[76] He cites various studies:

> "The most obvious, immediate conclusion is that the people do not work hard. The average length of time per person per day put into the appropriation and preparation of food was four or five hours. Moreover, they do not work continuously."[77]

> "The Bushman figures imply that one man's labor in hunting and gathering will support four or five people. Taken at face value, Bushman food collecting is more efficient than French farming in the period up to World War II. ... For each adult worker, this comes to about two and one-half days labor per week. ...A 'day's work' was about six hours."[78]

> "Reports suggest a mean of three to five hours per adult worker per day in food production. Hunters keep bankers' hours..."[79]

These days we have institutionalised hunger on an unprecedented scale, quite unlike the Old Stone Age. The industrial and commercial working week we have come to expect is not what humans faced through most of their evolutionary history. Production of food and many of the other goods of everyday life is a co-operative venture in hunter-gather societies. People do things with and for each other, exchange and give gifts. Sometimes this is casual and informal, sometimes highly organised, formal and even ritualised. The range of different forms of exchange is as varied as there are human cultures. Sometimes this exchange is local, within a family

---

[76] *ibid.* p. 1

[77] *ibid.* p.17

[78] *ibid.*p. 21

[79] *ibid. p. 35.*

group, and other times it may be more distant, as trade. Here are a couple of examples.

The !Kung bushmen of the Kalahari Desert

Although they live in a desert, the bushmen consider their homeland abundant and beautiful. They hunt various animals and gather a wide range of plant food. Their staple is the mongongo nut, which is easy to gather, and highly nutritious. In discussions with anthropologists it is clear that they were capable of planting the nuts, if they chose to do so. But one commented: "Why should we plant when there are so many mongongo nuts in the world?"[80]

Hunting is more difficult and less reliable than gathering. When a hunter kills an animal, it is his responsibility to divide it up among the members of the band. This is a socially complex act, guided by relationships, past giving, and precedent. Often a young man will seek the advice of his elders on it to ensure he does not commit a *faux pas*. In contrast, gathering of plant food is easy and is done by everyone. The food gathered is shared widely and casually.

The Trobriand Islanders and the Kula Ring[81]

For more settled groups, with simple agriculture, exchange is often more complex. The Trobriand Islands lie to the east of New Guinea. Much of the food of the islanders comes from shifting gardens, planted in different places in different years. There is a complex arrangement of ownership and use of these gardens. The *Towosi* (garden magician) supervises the clearing, planting and tending of the gardens. He initiates each stage of the gardening with a magical rite, which determines its timing. His expertise, expressed through the rituals he runs, thus ensures that everyone gets the best out of the land. Community members give ritual gifts to the *Towosi* as part of the ceremonies.

---

[80]Richard B Lee, "What hunters do for a living", in R.B. Lee, and I. DeVore, (eds.) *Man the Hunter*, Chicago, 1968, p. 33.

[81] Bronoslaw Malinowski, "The primitive economics of the Trobriand Islanders", *The Economic Journal*, March, 1921

"There are different systems of communal work on various scales; sometimes the several village communities join together, sometimes the whole community, sometimes a few households. ...In the more extensive kinds of work it is the chief's duty to feed the workers."[82]

There is a lot of redistribution of garden produce according to custom and ritual. This is a culture that is "enmeshed in a network of reciprocal obligations and dues, one constant flow of gift and counter-gift."

The chief is given ritual gifts of food on various occasions. He acts as a storehouse and redistributor. He can also transform food into objects of permanent wealth, through trade with other communities.

There was a trading system, called the Kula Ring, that included not just the Trobriand Islanders, but many other island communities to the east of New Guinea.[83] It was based on the exchange of two types of article of high value but of no real use – armshells and necklaces made of red shell-disks. Both were intended as ornaments but hardly used even for that purpose. Neither was kept for very long. Both travelled on a circular route, through trading partners with life-long relationships. An old chief might have a hundred trading partners, while a young commoner would have only a few. The necklaces travelled clockwise while the armshells travelled counter-clockwise along the trading routes. Thus in each trading pair one person would be giving the other armshells and receiving necklaces, while the other would give and receive the opposite.

The armshells and necklaces were in very limited supply. There was only a loose sense of the equivalence of the various valuables. The more valuable of them had individual names and histories and were known far and wide. The objective of the trade was to arrange to obtain the more prestigious ones from your trading partners. You in turn would soon pass them on to one of your other partners, thus obligating them to give you something prestigious in the future. To sweeten the trade, and to entice your partner to

---

[82] *ibid.* p. 7

[83] Bronoslaw Malinowski, "Kula; the circulating exchange of valuables in the archipelagoes of Eastern New Guinea", *Man*, July, 1920, pp. 97-105.

give the best objects to you, rather than to one of his other partners, all sorts of gifts were given as well. This included much more practical and useful items, such as pigs, yams and various other things. The trade enabled islands with agricultural surpluses to supply food to islands that had less food, but other useful objects.

This trade had very great practical benefits to the people that participated in it. However, from their point of view, it was the prestige of receiving high value Kula items that mattered socially, not the practical uses of the side gifts. There is a similarity here with our modern economy. In both cases, the medium of exchange (money for us, armshells and necklaces in the Kula ring) takes on primary importance and appears to be the purpose of the trade.

THE RECIPROCITY SPECTRUM

Sahlins classifies these forms of exchange along a spectrum, from what he calls generalised reciprocity, through balanced reciprocity, to negative reciprocity.[84]

- *'Generalised reciprocity'* includes the most altruistic forms – gifts, sharing, hospitality. However, generalised reciprocity is not simply a one-way transfer. There is an expectation of a return, but not on an immediate basis, or for a given item. So parents look after children who they expect to look after them when they are older. Such practices as 'kinship dues', 'chiefly dues' and 'noblesse oblige' are also examples of generalised reciprocity. Generalised reciprocity implies an on-going relationship between the people concerned. They are part of the same family, band or tribe. Today, this form of exchange is being discussed as 'the gift economy'.[85]

- *'Balanced reciprocity'* is the mid-point of the spectrum. The return is immediate. This includes modern money and markets, and also is the

---

[84] Marshall Sahlins, *op. cit.*. "On the sociology of primitive exchange", pp. 185-277.

[85] See, for example, Charles Eisenstein, <u>Sacred Economics</u>: <u>Money, Gift, and Society in the Age of Transition</u>.

classic form of barter and much of what involves 'primitive money'. It is less personal than generalised reciprocity, and involves a looser relationship.

- *'Negative reciprocity'* is "the unsociable extreme, ...the attempt to get something for nothing with impunity. ...The participants confront each other as opposed interests, each looking to maximise utility at the other's expense."[86] The extreme end of negative reciprocity is theft, rape and pillage. We also see it all the time in much of the market economy, and recently especially in the banking system.

For the !Kung bushmen, and most hunter-gather societies, exchange tends to be at the generalised end of the spectrum. In our modern economy, exchange tends to range between the balanced and negative ends of the spectrum. The eGaian image is of exchange that returns a long way towards the generalised end of the spectrum, helped by social networks and communications technology and a revival of the social skills needed, so that it retains the complexity and richness of the modern world.

---

[86] Marshall Sahlins, *op. cit.*. p. 195.

9 Towards the global cancer: the late human story

The origins and early history of humanity are about the ape that specialised in co-operative behaviour, developing language and culture as a means of enhancing our survival. Early humans lived a life to which they had evolved and adapted over nearly two million years. Their impact upon the natural world was comparable to that of other medium-sized mammals. Then, over a time period which is an evolutionary blink of an eye, humanity came to dominate the world, to have an impact which can be seen as a global cancer. This chapter traces that stage-by-stage transition. Recent research into the mechanisms of cancer shows that it too starts gradually:

> "Cancer begins deep inside the molecular machinery of a cell: first one genetic mutation, then another, and so on until the gene products that provide the usual checks and balances to cell division go awry, and the cell careers down the path of uncontrolled, cancerous proliferation."[87]

The course of humanity's global cancer shows a similar progressive loss of connection from the natural world and the checks and balances of evolution.

- With the development of settled living and agriculture, humanity started to become disconnected from the natural constraints on obtaining food, so its population could begin to rise.

- With the beginnings of civilisation and with it the transition from oral cultures to writing, human thought and spiritual life began to lose its intimate connection with natural processes. Wars, conflict and environmental destruction took a great spurt forward.

- With industrialisation came the change from wood and wind for energy to the use first of coal and later oil, gas and finally nuclear fuels. The

---

[87] Sylvia Wesphal, "Smart Bullets", *New Scientist*, No. 2319, 1 December 2001, p. 31-32.

natural constraints upon energy use began to be lost. The impacts of human technology could increase until they were large enough to change the climate and threaten the whole of the natural world.

- The final stage was reached in the late 20th century with the development of a globalised, commercially-dominated world economy. The constraints of local cultures were lost, and to a large extent those of national governments. Unending growth of production became the shrine and goal of public policy, with the preservation of the Earth an unpleasant side-issue that has to be coped with somehow. The warnings that we were reaching the limits of the Earth that started in the 1960s have begun to hit home in the first part of the 21st century.

Fortunately the possibility of a global eGaian culture was also established in that final stage. The world has become more multi-cultural than ever before, and people are connected through social networks and online media. This is our pre-adaptation to what could come. For the first time, there is the possibility of a new stage in evolution: self-awareness and co-ordination on a planetary scale.

You Hang on. Don't get carried away. And your potted history of human culture sounds a bit simplistic.

Me I'm sure it is hugely oversimplified. But let me spell out the four stages in a bit more detail.

DISCONNECTION FROM FOOD: SETTLED AGRICULTURE

This final chapter of the human story starts about 10,000 years ago, at the end of the last ice age. At the time, the total human population of the world was about 4 million. Then, for reasons that are not very clear, people began to lead more settled lives. They began to replace hunting with the domestication of animals and to replace gathering with crops they planted.

At one time it was thought "that the advantages of agriculture were so obvious that it must have been adopted as soon as human genius and invention had progressed far enough. Now such easy answers seem less plausible."[88] The hunter-gather life seems generally to have been easier. There was no need to plant, harvest and store crops. Agriculture relies on fewer crops so that in a bad year shortages and famine are more likely. Wilkinson speculates that rising populations led to a loss of 'ecological equilibrium'.[89] Perhaps the rising population was an over-reaction to the warmer, lusher conditions that appeared when the ice age ended. So here again, it may have been the response to a crisis that led to a breakthrough.

Agriculture seems to have developed independently in different parts of the world using different crops and animals. "The key centres were south-west Asia, China, Mesoamerica, the Andes and the tropical areas of Africa and south-east Asia."[90] Within these past 10,000 years it has spread throughout the world. Now very few hunter-gatherer societies remain, mostly in very isolated areas, usually with extremely small populations.

---

[88] Clive Ponting, *World History, A New Perspective*, Chatto and Windus, London, 2000, p. 51.

[89] Richard Wilkinson, *Poverty and Progress, An ecological model of economic development*, Methuen, London, 1973.

[90] Clive Ponting, *op. cit.* p. 51.

Whatever the reasons for its origins, once it became more highly developed, agriculture began to produce food surpluses. This meant that human populations could increase beyond the limitations of the carrying capacity of the land for gatherer-hunter societies. Humans had made a major break from the natural constraints on population for animals in the wild. The parallels with a cancer are clear.

The change from gatherer-hunter cultures to agriculture was a major one in physical ways for our co-operative ape. The diet and way of life that had shaped human physiology and psychology had changed substantially. The flesh of wild animals and fish is much less fatty than that of domesticated animals. Dairy products and grains as staples were new additions to the human diet. Not surprisingly, even today they are harder for us to digest than fruit and vegetables. For example, it is thought that for a person to retain the ability to digest milk after they are weaned is an adaptation that evolved in early cattle herders.[91] Most people, especially in southern Europe, Asia and Africa become intolerant to lactose after weaning.

> "Studies of today's few remaining traditional hunter-gather communities reveal a virtual absence of raised blood pressure, obesity, heart disease and diabetes in middle and late adulthood. This mismatch between our Pleistocene-attuned biology and our current way of life has been amplified over the past century as urban sedentariness, dietary excesses and various socialised addictive behaviours (alcohol consumption and tobacco smoking) have become prominent features of modern human ecology."[92]

DISCONNECTION IN THOUGHT AND SPIRIT: CIVILISATION

Early human cultures had a sense of connection with the natural world around them which is not at all part of the life experience of most people today. That disconnection took a great leap forward with the transition

---

[91] James Randerson, "Too old to take it", *New Scientist*, no. 2326, 19 January 2002.

[92] Tony McMichael, *Human Frontiers, Environments and disease*, Cambridge University Press, 2001, p.33.

from settled farming to civilisations. In many cases those early farming societies also became more hierarchical and unequal. Ponting takes up the story:

"Chiefs and religious authorities controlled much of the surplus food and redistributed it mainly in accordance with their priorities. As they did so they exercised more control over the people in their community. ...Societies at this level of development existed everywhere across the world for thousands of years..."

"In a handful of areas some societies... went much further and became coercive states and created the organisations, institutions and culture which we call civilisation. This process occurred at most six times in human history – in Mesopotamia, the Indus valley, China, Mesoamerica and the central Andes."

"These societies were distinguished by a number of features – they supported an elite of thousands of non-producers (priests, rulers, bureaucrats, craftsmen and warriors) who lived mainly in cities and who exercised power over the rest of the population through forms of taxation and tribute. ...Most developed some form of written script for various forms of record keeping."[93]

"The evolution of writing was central to the development of civilisation...it was fundamental to the functioning of the state in most early civilisations. Its purpose was not to represent a language but to store and transmit information. At first this was mainly about trade and administration..."

"Writing was central to the power of the state and the ability of it and the elite to control and exploit the majority of people."[94]

It was in these newly invented states, with their controlling elites, that the disconnection of thought and spirit began. David Abram, in *The Spell of the*

---

[93] *ibid.* p. 72.

[94] *ibid.* p. 102.

Sensuous[95], presents a persuasive picture of its origins. His thesis is that the change from oral cultures to cultures with writing (and especially alphabetic writing) was the key point of change.

Oral cultures perpetuate themselves through continually telling stories about their surroundings. Stories about specific locations and about plants and animals are crucial to their understanding of how to live. 'Spirits', as we call them, were not abstract, disembodied essences, in some other non-material realm, but aspects of the natural world around them. In their use of language, oral cultures participate in the world. "Here words do not speak *about* the world; rather they speak *to* the world, and to the expressive presences that, with us, inhabit the world." This is in contrast to "the character of linguistic discourse in the 'developed' or 'civilised' world, where language functions largely to deny reciprocity with nature – by defining the rest of nature as inert, mechanical, and determinate..."[96].

As writing progressed beyond record keeping to literature and philosophy, particularly in ancient Greece, this disconnection intensified. Oral culture, with its constantly repeated stories preserving cultural wisdom, became less and less important. People could look back at the written word, reflect on it and comment on it. This became the dominant way in which the culture was passed on. The evolution of human cultures had taken on a life of its own, no longer intimately tied to direct experience of the natural world.

People live in an environment shaped at least as much by ideas as by their direct experiences. These collections of ideas can regenerate and maintain themselves as they are passed from person to person. Once freed from the constraining bonds of nature, it was perhaps inevitable that all the features of the global cancer would eventually appear.

The practicalities of living in the early cities created a major disconnection from the natural world. Those who were not directly engaged with producing food were much less connected to it. Those who were, found that their activities and demands were increasingly determined by their

---

[95] David Abram, *The Spell of the Sensuous,* Vintage Books, 1997. A wonderful book!

[96] *ibid.* p. 71.

relationships with the others who controlled them. People began to rely on other people to provide much of what they needed. It was no longer the case that most people knew most of what there was to know in the culture. Most still worked on the land, but others specialised in producing implements, cloth, or in building or trade. This meant that people were no longer dealing directly with people they knew well.

Trade and barter became more important and money appeared. Money in the form of coins was said by Herodotus to have been first used in the 8th century BC. "They are the first people on record who coined gold and silver into money, and traded in retail."[97] The close coupling of producer and consumer had begun to loosen. Exchange had begun to move farther from the generalised end of Sahlins' reciprocity spectrum.

The sense of intimate support in the gathering-hunting band was no longer there. The earliest reports of widespread crime, corruption and dissolute youth come from the early civilisations. Professional fighters and standing armies appeared. Now there were groups of men whose principal function was to enforce the will of some groups on others. Wars on a much larger scale appeared. The technology of war took a huge leap forward in weaponry, military tactics and training. There were wars between gathering-hunting groups too, but they were conducted by men whose usual role in the culture was hunting and gathering. Those earlier wars were often highly ritualised, like much animal conflict. A war might end when the first blood was spilled.

Environmental problems appeared. Fertile land was farmed too intensively in places, creating deserts. Parts of northern Africa, now desert, were the granaries of the Roman Empire.

With all the social and political change came a new set of mythologies and world views. Authoritarian male gods and hierarchies of gods appeared, reflecting and justifying the political hierarchies in the early civilisations.

---

[97] Herodotus, *The Persian Wars, Book 1, Clio, 93*, translated by George Rawlinson, Modern Library, New York, 1942, p. 53.

The Earth mother goddess (the original incarnations of Gaia) and all the spirits of natural forces had lost their central place.

You So our global cancer really started with the beginning of civilisation? Are you saying it would it be better for the Earth if we all returned to that early hunter-gatherer lifestyle?

Me The size of the human population is far too great for the Earth to support us as gatherer-hunters. It is now about 1,500 times as large as it was at the end of the ice age, one measure of the extent of humanity as a global cancer. Moreover, I don't think it is remotely desirable from humanity's perspective. What I do think is possible is that we could regain the social intimacy and supportiveness of the most peaceful gatherer-hunter cultures while retaining a sophisticated technology, perhaps something like I described in the Pinecone Partnership story.

DISCONNECTED ENERGY AND TECHNOLOGY: INDUSTRIALISATION

The start of industrialisation in the 18th century marked another substantial increase in the impact of the global cancer, and of the disconnection between human cultures and the environment. The key to this increased impact was the development of new energy sources that enabled a huge growth and development of technology. In the 1750s agriculture occupied about 90% of the population. The relatively low productivity of agriculture limited the population overall and the proportion of the population that could be supported outside of agriculture. By the end of the 20th century, less than 5% of the population of the industrialised countries worked in agriculture.

The principal source of energy for agriculture up to the 18th century was human labour. Animals were used too, but humans ate less food. Supporting a horse required 4 or 5 acres of land. Oxen needed slightly less and so were the main draught animals. In 18th-century Europe there were about 24 million oxen and about 12 million horses.

"As late as 1806 one French agricultural writer could still advocate abandoning the plough and returning to digging fields by hand which although slower, was cheaper and more thorough."[98]

According to Ponting, industrialisation started first in England, not because it had increased its agricultural productivity but because it was able to import large quantities of food from its nearest colony – Ireland.[99] This, combined with the forcible eviction of peasants from their land by the big landlords, provided a workforce for the new industrial economy. Once started, the expansion of income from trade and increased imports from the colonies created a spiral of growth.

Waterpower was the main energy source for much early industry, with textile industries and other factories strung out along suitable rivers. In areas like the Netherlands, where waterpower was limited, wind was exploited. Wood was the main fuel until the 19th century. In the form of charcoal it was the primary industrial fuel for iron smelting, brewing, and glass making. It took a lot of woodland to fuel the early industrial revolution. An average small iron furnace used up about 250 acres of woodland every year. So industrial output was limited by the availability of what we now call renewable energy sources: human and animal power plus water, wind and wood.

Wood was also used for things like the construction of buildings, ships or furniture – so intensively that it became scarce. People had to make do with coal, considered a much inferior fuel at the time because it had to be mined and because it smelled bad when it burned.

"There is so great a scarcity of wood throughout the whole kingdom… the inhabitants in general are constrained to make their fires of sea-coal or pit-coal, even in the chambers of honourable personages."[100]

---

[98] Clive Ponting, *op. cit.* p. 646.

[99] *ibid*. p. 642.

[100] From Stow's *Annals of 1631*, quoted in Clive Ponting, *op. cit.*p. 648.

Once again, a change was adopted not because it was seen as an advance but because of a crisis in the older system. Once adopted, the new fuel opened new horizons. The growth of human industry was no longer constrained by the available energy from renewable sources. All of those were obtained indirectly from current sunlight falling on the Earth. Now energy was obtained from ancient sunlight, from forests that grew about 300 million years ago. This was the beginning of human ability to pollute the Earth on a grand scale. As coal was followed by oil and then gas as major fuels, more and more ancient forests were burned. Ancient carbon that had been removed from the atmosphere was returned as carbon dioxide. This was the beginning of global warming. The global cancer was getting large enough to change the Earth's climate.

In the early stages of industrialisation, the pollution from released carbon dioxide was insignificant compared to the more obvious pollution of the newly expanded industry.

> "By the nineteenth century across Europe and North America there were areas of concentrated pollution and environmental degradation – ruined landscapes of chimneys belching smoke and poisonous gases, huge slag heaps of waste materials, rivers full of a cocktail of industrial wastes and surrounding areas where the vegetation was destroyed."[101]

There were many other changes as well. The modern world was taking shape. Cities became much more important, What had been trading centres and a focus for the rich and their courts were now centres of industrial production. Transport and communications improved, first with the development of canals and then, once the steam engine arrived, the railways. Governments took on new functions. Before that their main function was military. Now, with the new urban cultures, with a new class of industrial poor, and all the new industries, they added policing and prisons, regulation of industries (especially the strategically important railways), provision of water and sanitation in the new cities.

---

[101] *ibid.* p. 668

There were major changes in political control too. Between 1750 and 1900 Europe came to dominate the rest of the world. In 1800 Europe controlled about a third of the world's land surface, in 1900 over four-fifths. The stage was now set for the final chapter in this story – globalisation.

THE DISCONNECTED ECONOMY: GLOBALISATION

The human story in the 20th century – especially in its second half – is of the cancer reaching its limits. With globalisation, human intervention on the natural world lost its remaining constraints, those of local cultures and governments. The driving force for most human enterprise has become the pursuit of monetary flows, an abstraction quite free from physical and biological constraints. Our impact on the natural world became so large that changes in weather patterns and climate became noticeable, and not just a scientific prediction, while the undermining of wilderness areas, fisheries and soil fertility is catastrophic.

The state of food production illustrates the situation. At the beginning of the 20th century, most agriculture worldwide was for local consumption. Local food was adapted to local conditions, so that every region had its specialities, season by season. Soil fertility depended almost entirely on manures and composts produced on the farm. But in the second half of the 20th century, food and farming became just one more industry, now using industrial techniques to improve the money flows through the industry. Through the use of farm machinery, the number of people required in agriculture dropped drastically. The use of larger machines led to larger fields and increasing dependence upon single crops, which were more susceptible to diseases and pests, and so were kept in check by chemical herbicides and pesticides. Productivity was increased by the use of chemical fertilisers. "The soil was treated less as a living organism and more as a medium to hold crops in position as more and more chemicals were poured on to them."[102]

---

[102] *ibid.* p. 790.

As an eminently marketable product, food developed in ways that enhanced its profitability rather than its effect on the health of people or the land. So highly processed foods appeared, with additives to prolong their shelf life. Fruit and vegetables lost their seasonal round. Limited numbers of standardised varieties are now shipped all over the world, replacing local varieties. Freshness, flavour and nutritional value take a poor second place to pristine appearance and suitability to industrial farming and distribution. High margin junk foods are the most heavily promoted. When did you last see a TV advertisement for fresh vegetables? Supermarket layout and design is a highly developed science; you can get PhDs in it. Atmosphere, lighting and smells are all carefully designed to put you in a receptive mood. Go into a supermarket in most industrial countries and you will find yourself in familiar territory.

Of course food is marketable only to people who have money. So land in Asia, Africa and South America came to be used to grow crops for export, leaving only the worst land for the poorer local populations. The result is a world in which billions go hungry while food is in plentiful supply. A domestic cat in the United States eats more meat than the average inhabitant of Africa and Latin America.

And it's not just food that has become globalised. During the early part of the industrial revolution wealthy individuals and families owned the new factories, mills and then the big retail outlets. They were still part of the local culture. The middle of the 20th century saw the rise of multi-national corporations which changed that completely. Professional managers began to run the corporations, and financial institutions – banks, insurance companies and pension funds – owned their stock. As global transport and communications improved, it became possible and desirable (financially) to run a company that was distributed throughout the world. In the 1960s the Ford Motor Company in Britain made the Cortina for British use. In the 1980s its replacement, the Escort was designed for the European market and assembled in three plants incorporating parts made in 15 countries.

Large companies are now many of the largest economic organisations, dwarfing the economies of all but the largest nations. National governments have a very limited ability to influence them, as large companies threaten to move their production elsewhere. On the contrary, governments woo companies, offering financial inducements and freedom from social and environmental restrictions to locate in their territories.

Perhaps the clearest sign of how disconnected the human economy has become is what has happened to the financial markets. Before globalisation, the buying and selling of currencies was a necessary service to the rest of the economy. Now currency trading totally dominates world trade. With the abandonment of the gold standard by the US in 1970 and then the deregulation of currency transactions in the 1980s, all limits were removed. As late as the 1970s, the typical daily volume of foreign currency transactions was in the range of $10-20 billion. On a normal day in 2000 that had risen to $2,000 billion. This amounts to over 150 times the total daily international trade of all commodities and services worldwide.[103] This is speculative trading, whose purpose is to make a profit from the changes in value of the currency. As John Maynard Keynes said:

> "Speculators may do no harm as bubbles on a steady stream of enterprise. But the position is serious when enterprise becomes the bubble on a whirlpool of speculation. When the capital development of a country becomes a by-product of the activities of a casino, the job is likely to be ill-done."[104]

With a cancer, unlimited expansion is all that matters. From the point of view of the growing cancer cells, it might seem great, "Our empire is expanding!" But from the point of view of the body, it means death and, ultimately, death to the cancer cells as well. All of humanity is currently caught up in the out-of-control, unlimited expansion that is our global cancer. Much of the problem is an unwillingness to look deeply enough and question the nature of our society.

---

[103] Bernard Lietar, *The Future of Money*, Century, London, 2001.

[104] John Maynard Keynes, *The General Theory of Employment, Interest and Money*, Macmillan, London, 1936.

THE POSSIBILITY OF EGAIA

Fortunately, as the cancer has reached its global limits it has also brought with it the possibilities of overcoming it. Several of the changes that made globalisation possible are also essential to a re-connection.

The late 20th century forced upon us a global view: a growth in environmental awareness, an awareness of humanity-as-a-whole through multi-culturalism and global television, some halting attempts at a framework for global peace, and most recently, a communications infrastructure which can enable humanity to function as a global nervous system, should it choose to do so. These possibilities form the contents of parts 3 and 4. Can we re-connect:

- with food, restoring our physiological link to the natural world;
- in energy, so that we allow the Earth's climate to recover or at least stabilise;
- in our economy, so that we act to promote the health of humanity and the natural world;
- in thought and spirituality, so that we begin to form a single, global family that could be eGaia?

PART 3 AN EGAIAN GUIDE: PHILOSOPHY AND PRINCIPLES

10 eGaian relationships

The starting point for eGaia is developing co-operative rather than competitive relationships with others. This is necessary if we are to see ourselves as part of a larger whole, the living Earth. This requires an understanding of the communications principles necessary for co-operation. This chapter explores these ideas by going back to first principles: how we construct the personal worlds in which we each live. Further chapters of Part 3 apply that kind of relationship in wider contexts – to conflict resolution, to a sustainable Earth and to a co-operative economy.

THE RELATIONSHIP SPECTRUM

What does it mean for the Earth to function with the coherence of an organism with humanity analogous to its nervous system? The primary characteristic of an organism is its wholeness: its parts do not act independently; they act in support of the whole and thus in support of each other. At a personal level, this implies a shift in relationships from competition towards mutual support and collaboration. That change of relationship is a shift along a spectrum, as in the diagram below.

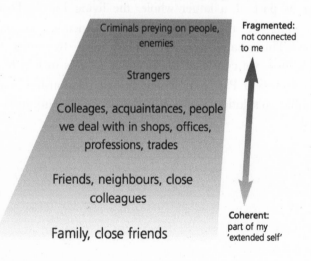

Relationships at the near end of this spectrum are 'coherent' in contrast to 'fragmented'. Relationships at the coherent end are close, loving and supportive, those at the fragmented end are distant, coercive and difficult. At the coherent end are people who are like an extension of oneself. At the fragmented end, people are disconnected.

> **You** But I know lots of people who hate other members of their families.

> **Me** Sure, but it is the qualities of relationship in this spectrum that I'm trying to clarify. The fact that there are many exceptions is not the point.

What is it that changes along this spectrum?

- the degree to which people identify with each other, as part of a sort of 'extended self';
- the degree to which people understand each other, from the other's point of view, and the way this leads to acceptance and tolerance of differences.

As will become clear later in the chapter, to maintain a relationship at the coherent end of the spectrum, it helps to have communication strategies that can resolve or at least diffuse the conflicts that inevitably arise.

To begin to clarify this relationship spectrum, here is a fairly extended set of examples, which later sections will draw on. It starts at the fragmented end.

Professional burglars, thieves and muggers Crime is one of the world's largest industries. When someone snatches your bag, chances are they don't think of you as a person like themselves, any more than a lion feels compassion for the gazelle it kills. You are 'other', something that doesn't matter to them. They don't hate you, and aren't angry with you. You, the person, simply don't come into their awareness. They can sustain this as a way of life, largely because they are part of a sub-culture in which it is acceptable, regardless of what the rest of society says.

Cultures at war The Arab-Israeli conflict is one of many similar examples of cultures at war at present. The next chapter, on conflict resolution, uses it as an example, but the essence of the argument. between the two sides is depressingly familiar to all. Outsiders may see a spiral of violence – the actions of both sides are taken by the other side as justifying their own violence and even making it necessary – but each side takes a more limited view. Their own anger and pain blinds them to the suffering they are inflicting on the other side, who they demonise. They see themselves as victims of the other side, not as part of a process in which both sides are the cause of the other side's violence.

Strangers meeting casually *Fear:* you walk past a strange-looking group of people in the evening on an empty street in a large town. You think to yourself, "Am I about to be attacked?" You walk on past. There is no eye contact, no exchange of greetings. You continue to walk in fear for quite a while.

Casual friendship You walk in a wild, hilly place with a group of friends, and you encounter another group of walkers. You pass, you say "Hello!" and "What a beautiful day!" and walk on, never to see each other again. The entire relationship is brief but pleasant. The words and the body language say "I am not a threat, my intentions are friendly. You and I are people who like the same kinds of things."

Hospitality to strangers Many cultures have had very strong traditions of hospitality to strangers. "When in 1568 a European missionary arrived out of the blue at Nagasaki, he was given a Buddhist temple to stay in, and banquets three nights running... The Lithuanian word for guest is clansman (svetjas), because by eating and sleeping in another's house, a guest became a member of his host's clan. In Albania, a host who gave hospitality to a stranger was obliged to take revenge on anyone who harmed him before he reached his next destination."[105]

The people in the shops There's a shop selling electrical and electronic goods, staffed by bright young men wearing the shop's shirt and tie. They don't know anything about you and they don't ask. They show you several models and sing the praises of one of the more expensive ones. Do they get

---

[105] Theodore Zeldin, *An Intimate History of Humanity*, Vintage, 1998, p. 437.

more commission on that one, or is it really better? Can you trust them? Are they serving you or themselves? There's another shop where several of your friends work. Whenever you walk in you get a nice greeting but sometimes have to forestall long conversations if you are busy. You know their advice is, at the worst, their view of your best interests.

Creative arts camp This is an example of ordinary Western people meeting under circumstances which bring out the best and most co-operative within them.

There may be as many as several hundred people, a lot of them children, at the camp. People come expecting to camp in a circle around a common campfire with some friends. Each camping circle usually unites more than one group of friends and some newcomers and become instant communities. They are memorable social units. People will say, "You remember so and so. They were in such and such's circle, over by the grove, two years ago." People come from various backgrounds and income levels, but share a love of music and of these camps. The setting is conducive to creating friendships. There are many tasks to share – cooking, tending the fire, looking after the children – and activities to go to together. Most of the routine tasks of looking after the camp as a whole are spread out among the campers, working half a day each, in a fairly organised way. Crews of campers keep the toilets clean, work in the café and the children's area. The camp would be much more expensive if people had to be paid to do that.

Over the years, a culture and tradition of the camps has grown up which is passed on to newcomers – so they find a sense of instant community, created effortlessly. Many people find the camps very powerful experiences, and want more like that in their lives.

The happy couple Despite all the broken families and dysfunctional relationships, there are still many relationships that do work well, and they form a fitting end to the relationship spectrum. The happy couple know that the other's mood can make a difference to their own mood, so it is self-interest as well as love which leads them to act to support the other's happiness. They are very aware of the practical and emotional benefits of having someone to share their lives with.

They spend a fair proportion of their time together, but also have quite separate lives and interests. Both respect their partners' independent time and enjoy hearing about it. The differences between them lead them to have quite different views on some subjects. (This is sometimes to do with very personal aspects of their life, such as tidiness and hygiene, food, dress, etc.) They know that these differences are inevitable, and generally enjoy and accept them light-heartedly. They feel that this acceptance and tolerance is a major strength of their relationship.

When the differences between them begin to cause tension, (as it must from time to time) they have learned strategies for diffusing it. Lateral thinking is often a useful way out of conflict. They find some solution that satisfies both of them. Neither is shy about complaining, having found that the other generally listens with sympathy and tends to take the complaint on board. Their mutual acceptance and tolerance leads to low defensiveness.

They share some of their income, but not all. Their contributions to their joint expenses are roughly the same, but they don't worry about trying to keep careful records or about getting it exactly equal. It isn't worth the effort, and besides, they like doing things to please each other.

> **You** So you think all relationships should aim to become like the happy couple? I don't want to spend my time hearing all about the personal lives of the people I meet in shops, and doubt if I will ever come to love them.

> **Me** No, I didn't say that. Everyone has relationships in many different parts of the spectrum. All I am suggesting is a shift along it. I am trying to tease out what the crucial differences are along the spectrum so we can create the conditions for coherent rather than fragmented relationships.

SELVES AND EXTENDED SELVES

> *"A human being is part of the whole, called by us 'Universe', a part limited in time and space. He experiences himself, his thoughts and feelings as something*

separated from the rest – a kind of optical delusion of his consciousness. This delusion is a kind of prison for us, restricting us to our personal desires and to affection for a few persons nearest to us. Our task must be to free ourselves from this prison by widening our circle of compassion to embrace all living creatures and the whole nature in its beauty." Albert Einstein[106]

A good starting point for looking more deeply at this relationship spectrum is to look at our sense of self and how we create it. Our bodies are the most obvious first look at who we are. Alan Watts calls this "the skin-encapsulated ego." We learn to see ourselves as our bodies in infancy as we become aware of our separateness from our mothers and our surroundings. A baby gradually comes to be able to control its body. It learns to control its limbs. It learns to give signs that result in its being fed, so satisfying internal needs. The sense of what is 'me' grows by contrast with what is 'not me'. I can bang my fist, but that table resists my banging. It is 'not me'. Thus begins a sense of 'me' as 'that which I am able to control and look after'.

This early psychological sense of self closely parallels the physical organisation of the body as a control system.[107] Our bodies control their internal temperature to within a fraction of a degree. They control and preserve the chemical composition of the blood and tissues very accurately. To enable the internal, unconscious parts of us to do this, our overall conscious part must behave in suitable ways. It must control the limbs to put clothes on and off to help maintain its temperature. It must act in ever more complex ways to ensure a suitable supply of food, shelter and other physical needs.

Peter Russell contrasts 'the skin-encapsulated ego' with a broader sense of self as "unbounded, part of a greater wholeness, united with the rest of the Universe."[108]

---

[106] Quoted in Peter Russell, *The Awakening Earth, Our Next Evolutionary Leap*, Routledge & Kegan Paul, 1982.

[107] A wonderful book describing the body, and especially the brain, as a control system, is William T. Powers, *Behavior: The Control of Perception*, Wildwood House, London, 1974.

108 Peter Russell, *op. cit.* p. 115.

This book proposes a related but more limited sense of extended self as a starting point while keeping Peter's vision in mind philosophically.

My study as my shell

As I sit at my desk in my study, an environment surrounds me that has been mostly shaped by me. The books, messy desk, ornaments, pictures on the wall all give anyone entering the room a strong sense of me, my interests and personality. Just as I eat, exercise, dress, etc to keep my body healthy, I act to keep my study as it suits me. It is part of what I care about and look after.

Even in the animal kingdom, 'the organism' may mean more than 'the physical body'. Is the shell of a snail part of the snail or part of its environment? What about a bee hive? Scott Turner, in *The Extended Organism*[109] makes the case that the structures animals build should be properly considered to be external organs of physiology.

We can use the term 'extended self' to reflect this internal, psychological sense of self, as 'that which you care about and look after'. So in this sense, your immediate family and close friends are generally part of your extended self. You may do a lot for your children, at great personal cost, because they are part of what you care about. Similarly, your personal possessions and home are part of your extended self. (People feel violated when their home or car is broken into, even though they haven't been physically harmed themselves.)

There are wider, but perhaps less intense aspects of the extended self, like your values and those aspects of your community, your culture or the world which you care about. When you give money to relieve a famine on the other side of the world you are seeing the people there as a part of your extended self in a small way. If you are upset when you read of a genocidal war or the destruction of a rainforest, those people and that forest are, at least momentarily, part of your extended self.

---

109 J. Scott Turner, *The Extended Organism*, Harvard University Press, 2000.

Going back to the relationship spectrum, it is clear that the Arabs and Israelis are not part of each other's extended selves. Nor are the burglar's victims. With friendly and hospitable strangers a little extended self begins to creep in, as it certainly does in the friendly shop. The creative arts camp is set up in such a way as to encourage people to see each other as parts of their extended selves, as it is expected that they will be looking after each other. And of course, the lives of the happy couple are so intertwined that the old cliché 'my other (better?) half' certainly applies.

Thus anything which encourages people to see each other (and also the natural world) as part of their extended self is a step towards an eGaian world. This includes much of the environmental movements and peace movements, and many of the experiments with new forms of community (*kibbutzim*, communes and co-operatives) of the past century. The message from the creative arts camp is that it is possible to set up new structures in which people naturally find themselves seeing each other as part of their extended self. Social structures that do that will form the basis of the steps towards an eGaian world.

THE VIEW FROM INSIDE: CONSTRUCTING ONE'S WORLD

> **Me:** The following starts abstract and philosophical but leads to intensely practical results.

To fully understand the sense of self we need to understand how an individual 'constructs their world', from the inside. For example…

Sitting in my garden...

I sit in my garden writing this book. If I reflect superficially as to what my world is at the moment, I might say it is what I see and hear around me: the house, the garden and beyond, shapes I recognise as flowers, bushes, walls and windows. I hear birds, wind, traffic and other people in the distance.

But looking a little closer, there is much more to it than that. I experience a mixture of emotions: excitement, a little fear and impatience with myself for being so slow. Thoughts are tumbling through my mind, some related to the book, others to various other aspects of my life: chores I have to do, my next meal, my partner. I live in an almost incessant stream of 'words-in-my-head' that flits about from one sub-stream to the next.

My primary reality, my personal 'View' is that continuous and subjective jumble of thoughts, feelings and perceptions. My physical surroundings and body are just a part of it. They are secondary, something I sometimes pay attention to.

I take a sip of tea from my favourite mug and experience the familiar taste and feelings of relaxation I associate with cups of tea. My experience of drinking tea includes elements of all previous cups of tea I have drunk and the social situations in which I have had them. My enjoyment of the design of the mug is there too. The present-moment physical sensations are only a small part of the experience.

So our starting point is this fundamental experience that it is our private and subjective 'View' of the world which is our primary reality. Our experience of the physical world is secondary. It is constructed out of that View. [110]

The construction of a person's View is an active process. It is not simply the mixture of thought and perception that determines experience. Your View seems like a detailed, seamless world, as though it were being recorded by a video camera. Actually, your perception is very limited. The full information you would need to receive all the shapes, movement and sounds around you to really experience that detailed, seamless world is vastly beyond the capacity of your senses. Moreover, your brain would need a lot more information processing power than it has to make sense of it all. Instead, what happens is that you continually guess what is going to

---

[110] This is a superficial introduction to a very deep subject. For a very clear discussion of the primacy of consciousness see Peter Russell's *From Science to God, The Mystery of Consciousness and the Meaning of Light*, New World Library, 2005.

happen next. Your mind anticipates what will happen from its past experiences. It fills in most of the missing information from what it expects.

Sometimes that process of seamless construction breaks down and you become aware of it.

The time I shouted at my trousers

I went into the bedroom early one evening and spotted a shape on the bed. In the half-light I wasn't instantly sure what it was, but I suddenly thought, "The dog is on the bed!" The size was about right and I could just about recognise its head, ears and tail. I shouted "Get off!" as I had a long-standing policy that the dog was not allowed on the bed I slept in. I rushed forward to enforce my will, switched on the light, and broke out in laughter. On the bed were my trousers, jumbled up as I had left them earlier. In the light they looked nothing like the dog, but my memory is clear: In the half-light I 'saw' the head, ears and tail.

The step that wasn't there

I was leaving the home of good friends whom I had visited before. The outside light bulb had failed, but the path was familiar to me. There were several steps down, around a dark corner where I couldn't see. I walked down the first three steps confidently, but on the fourth 'step' I stumbled and nearly fell. My memory had failed me. There were only three steps. My body movements, anticipating a fourth step that wasn't there, were completely inappropriate to level ground.

Misheard names on the telephone

Have you ever noticed that if someone answers the telephone with their own name as the first word ("Richard speaking..."), it is impossible to understand? It takes a few words for you to key into the characteristics of another person's voice. Only then can you anticipate the next words and thus recognise them. A name doesn't have enough context to allow you to do this. If you pay attention to what you actually can remember when you hear a new name on the phone then you will get a clue as to how much of your 'experience' is actually filled in by your anticipation.

Making a light switch vanish

Here is a party trick. You can make a light switch or any small object on a plain wall appear to vanish by using the blind spot in your eye. Locate a small object on a plain wall opposite you. Put your right hand over your right eye. Then extend your left hand and point to the object with your left forefinger. While concentrating on your finger, move your left hand to the right very slowly. After you have moved your hand about six inches to the right the object will seem to vanish. It will be in the blind spot of your left eye and you will see a continuous blank wall. For this to work you have to avoid the temptation to look directly at the object. Keep looking at your finger, but notice when the object disappears from view. Your mind does not allow you to experience a hole in your perception. It fills in the details from the clues it has available, in this case the surrounding wall.

> **Yes** That seems like a clever trick, and I will try it, but what is the point you are getting at? What does this have to do with people trying to collaborate?
>
> **Me** Much of what we think we are experiencing, that is, stuff coming from 'out there' is actually our minds filling in details from what we expect to experience. This can fool us when we are dealing with other people. Haven't you ever found that you thought you had an understanding with someone who later claimed to see it much differently than you? Often we think we agree with someone on the basis of brief comments. We have filled in a lot of agreement that was never really there. A lot of careful checking of agreement is needed.

So you can't make sense of a person's View simply by looking at their external circumstances. From the outside, it might seem as though they should be happy, should believe certain things, should choose certain actions. From their internal perspective it could look completely different. It is perfectly reasonable for two people to have what an observer might think was the same experience and yet have a completely different understanding of it. Each is actually taking in different aspects and filling out their construction based upon their own past history and expectations.

First principle of a coherent relationship

Both people must attempt to understand each other from each other's perspective, from each others' View.

It follows from this is that you cannot make sense of another person's View without sufficient communication to know what that View is.

To summarise the argument so far, we live in our View, our private subjective reality that consists of a mixture of feelings, thoughts and perceptions. At any moment, memories of many similar events are evoked by our current perceptions. We use these to make sense of the present moment and to anticipate what will happen next. Without that anticipation, very little of our perceptions would be understandable. There is just too much coming in at any one time to make sense of it otherwise.

CONVERGENT COMMUNICATION: KNOWING THAT YOU ARE IN AGREEMENT

Everyone has had experiences where they thought they had an agreement with someone else and later found that wasn't the case. It may have been on some personal level such as an arrangement on where and when to meet. It may be an understanding with someone you work for, or with someone offering you a service. Sometimes you might be convinced that the other person has knowingly distorted the agreement, but sometimes it is clear that both genuinely saw it in different ways.

This is where the idea that our View is our primary reality becomes so powerful. Differences in View need not be seen as contradictory. They can be perfectly consistent within the context of each person's different experience and anticipation.

Here is a comical story that was circulating on the Internet. Ignore the dreadful gender stereotypes and enjoy the way two very different Views are formed out of a joint experience.

The differences between men and women

Let's say a guy named Roger is attracted to a woman named Elaine. He asks her out to a movie; she accepts; they have a pretty good time. A few nights later he asks her out to dinner, and again they enjoy themselves. They continue to see each other regularly, and after a while neither one of them is seeing anybody else.

And then, one evening when they're driving home, a thought occurs to Elaine, and without really thinking, she says it aloud: "Do you realise that, as of tonight, we've been seeing each other for exactly six months?" And then there is silence in the car. To Elaine, it seems like a very loud silence. She thinks to herself: "Geez, I wonder if it bothers him that I said that? Maybe he's feeling confined by our relationship; maybe he thinks I'm trying to push him into some kind of obligation that he doesn't want, or isn't sure of?" And Roger is thinking: "Gosh, six months."

Elaine is thinking: "But hey, I'm not so sure I want this kind of relationship either. Sometimes I wish I had a little more space, so I'd have time to think about whether I really want us to keep going the way we are, moving steadily towards... I mean, where are we going? Are we just going to keep seeing each other at this level of intimacy? Are we heading towards marriage? Toward children? Toward a lifetime together? Am I ready for that level of commitment? Do I really even know this person?" And Roger is thinking: "...so that means it was... let's see... February when we started going out, which was right after I had the car at the dealer's, which means... lemme check the odometer. ...Whoa! I am way overdue for an oil change here."

Elaine is thinking: "He's upset. I can see it on his face. Maybe I'm reading this completely wrong. Maybe he wants more from our relationship, more intimacy, more commitment; maybe he has sensed — even before I sensed it — that I was feeling some reservations. Yes, I bet that's it. That's why he's so reluctant to say anything about his own feelings. He's afraid of being rejected." And Roger is thinking: "And I'm going to have them look at the transmission again. I don't care what those morons say, it's still not shifting right. And they better not try to blame it on the cold weather this time. What cold weather? It's 87 degrees out, and this thing is shifting like a goddamn garbage truck, and I paid those incompetent thieves $600."

Elaine is thinking: "He's angry. And I don't blame him. I'd be angry too. God, I feel so guilty, putting him through this, but I can't help the way I feel. I'm just not sure." And Roger is thinking: "They'll probably say it's only a 90-day warranty. That's exactly what they're gonna say, the scumballs."

Elaine is thinking: "Maybe I'm just too idealistic, waiting for a knight to come riding up on his white horse, while I'm sitting right next to a perfectly good person, a person I enjoy being with, a person I truly do care about, a person who seems to truly care for me. A person who is in pain because of my self-centred, schoolgirl romantic fantasy." And Roger is thinking: "Warranty? They want a warranty I'll give them a goddamn warranty. I'll take their warranty and stick it right up their…

"Roger" Elaine says aloud. "What?" asks Roger, startled. "Please don't torture yourself like this," she says, her eyes beginning to brim with tears. "Maybe I should never have… Oh God, I feel so… " (She breaks down, sobbing.) "What?" says Roger.

"I'm such a fool," Elaine sobs. "I mean, I know there's no knight. I really know that. It's silly. There's no knight, and there's no horse." "There's no horse?" asks Roger.

"You think I'm a fool, don't you?" Elaine says. "No!" says Roger, glad to finally know the correct answer.

"It's just that… It's just that… I need some time." Elaine says. (There is a 15-second pause while Roger, thinking as fast as he can, tries to come up with a safe response. Finally he comes up with one that he thinks might work.) "Yes" he says.

(Elaine, deeply moved, touches his hand.) "Oh Roger, do you really feel that way?" "What way?" says Roger.

155

"That way about time." says Elaine. "Oh" says Roger, "Yes."

(Elaine turns to face him and gazes deeply into his eyes, causing him to become very nervous about what she might say next, especially if it involves a horse. At last she speaks.) "Thank you Roger." she says. "Thank you" says Roger.

Then he takes her home, and she lies on her bed, a conflicted, tortured soul and weeps until dawn, whereas when Roger gets back to his place, he opens a bag of Doritos, turns on the TV and immediately becomes deeply involved in a rerun of a tennis match between two Czechoslovakians he never heard of. A tiny voice in the far recesses of his mind tells him that something major was going on back there in the car, but he is pretty sure there is no way he would ever understand what, and so he figures it's better if he doesn't think about it. (This is also Roger's policy regarding world hunger.)

The next day Elaine will call her closest friend, or perhaps two of them, and they will talk about this situation for six straight hours, never reaching any definite conclusions, but never getting bored with it either. Roger, while playing racquetball one day with a mutual friend of his and Elaine's, will pause just before serving, frown and ask: "Norm, did Elaine ever own a horse?"

This story illustrates how easily people's Views may become very different, even when they have what might appear to be a shared experience. Each is paying attention to different things. Both are dominated by their internal worlds, not the few actual words that pass between them. Even the words don't have the same meaning to both of them.

This potential for Views to diverge doesn't mean that communication and mutual understanding are impossible. It simply means that they cannot be taken for granted. Careful checking is needed to confirm agreement and to probe the limits of agreement.

During the last century, with the growth of new communications media, engineers had to develop means for machines to communicate reliably with each other. They were faced with the ever-present possibility that noise, interference and bad connections would corrupt messages. They developed principles for understanding the process of communication in the abstract, away from the messy emotional details of human communication.

So, how do two computers 'know' they 'understand' each other? When computers connect to each other through the Internet they exchange data in discrete packets. Each packet is coded in such a way that errors can be detected. After each packet is sent, there is a 'handshake' to confirm that the packet has been accurately received. If not, the packet is re-sent and re-sent until the sending computer gets a message that confirms to it that the packet has been correctly received.

This continual checking for errors has been found necessary for machine communication to be reliable. People with good communications skills (not Elaine and Roger) often do the equivalent intuitively. Because language is so basic to being human we often take for granted that we are being understood. And we often find that we are wrong in that. As in the joke above, a conversation can simply be a series of exchanges of words, where neither side has any idea whether the other has understood them. Fortunately, much human communication does a lot better than that. For example, one person may speak while the other listens and replies occasionally with nods, grunts or whatever. These may be a rough equivalent of the computer's checking of a packet.

> **You** Or they might just be pretence at listening.

> **Me** True, but someone who is skilled at communicating will make regular indications that they are following and understanding, and will ask questions when they aren't.

The telecommunications engineers' principles can be applied more explicitly to human discussions and can make it much more reliable too. The engineers have identified a basic communications cycle: sending some information and checking that it has been understood. We can take that as a basic unit of human communications too. Communication then becomes not just a series of statements but rather a series of: [statements plus checking that it is understood]. The illustration below shows the process.

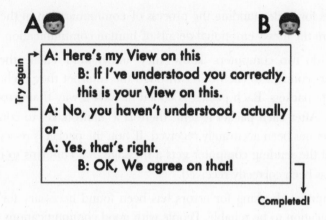

A 👦   **B** 👧

Try again

A: Here's my View on this
    B: If I've understood you correctly,
    this is your View on this.
A: No, you haven't understood, actually
or
A: Yes, that's right.
    B: OK, We agree on that!

Completed!

Let's unpick the various bits of this cycle:

- 'Here's my View of this.' is the statement A hopes B will understand. The rest is designed to check that it has been understood.

- In the second line, person B is reflecting back, from B's perspective, what B thinks A was saying (from A's perspective). This is quite different from either agreeing or disagreeing with A. The crucial point is that B is trying to see from A's perspective, to reflect back A's full View, not just A's words.

- In the third line, A isn't continuing the discussion. A is simply clarifying whether B has or has not understood. If not, A tries again, perhaps in somewhat different words.

- Finally, when A indicates agreement, B confirms it. Then both can be as confident as possible that they have reached agreement.

In a casual conversation, often nothing rides on the outcome. People may simply be passing time rather than looking for agreement. In that case, this cycle is not needed. The usual grunts etc will do to at least indicate that the listener is listening. In more serious circumstances, as when joint action is planned, a loose informal version of the communications cycle is a good idea. ("So long, see you at 5 tomorrow at the café", "I thought you said 5:30." "No, it was 5." "OK")

When the communication really counts, for example in tense emotional situations, a skilled communicator will use the communications cycle in full, repeatedly. They will make sure that they see the other person's perspective and have understood as fully as possible what the other intends and that the other knows that before moving on to the next point in the discussion.

Another important part of the telecommunications engineer's conceptual repertoire is to see the communications process in terms of layers or levels.

- At the lowest levels are the physical connections. What types of wires, plugs and sockets, voltage and current levels does a system use?
- At somewhat higher levels are the conventions and protocols used. How long are the packets and how are they put together? What codes should be used for checking and correcting errors?
- At still higher levels there is the content of the communication: your email messages, a picture you are downloading from the Web.

This concept of 'levels of communication' also applies to human communication. In the communications cycle described above there is the main statement which is the content of the discussion. The rest of the cycle has the function of checking that it has been understood. That checking process is part of the next level up. It is communication about the communication process.

In the story of Elaine and Roger, Elaine looks at Roger's face and body language to gauge his reaction. Again, this is the second level: monitoring the state of the discussion, this time using clues about emotional state. Elaine doesn't get it right because she doesn't check it, but at least she is using that level whereas Roger is not. Elaine gets upset because she thinks her remark has endangered the relationship. This concern about whether the relationship is converging or diverging is the third level. The third level is communication about the second level, whether it is succeeding or not.

To summarise these three levels:

- At the basic level is the content of the discussion. It consists of the main messages each person is trying to convey to the other.

- The next level is communication about the discussion. It includes body language and tone of voice.
- The third level is communication about the second level and is simply concerned about whether the conversation is converging (going well) or diverging (going badly).

Skilful communicators make good use of the three levels. They will remain aware of them at all times. If they think that there is misunderstanding at the level of the content they will move to the second level, checking that there is agreement. They may use the communications cycle explicitly, working to make sure the other person feels understood in terms of their own View. If a discussion seems to be going badly, they may appeal to the third level: "Hey, I thought we were friends! I really don't want this discussion to spoil that." "We seem to be continually talking across each other. I really want us to end up with a solution we can both agree upon."

Second principle of a coherent relationship

A coherent relationship must be based on convergent communication. Both people must make an effort to be sure they are understood. They must regularly ensure that their views haven't diverged too much.

Coherent relationships, based upon convergent communication, are the basis of an eGaian world. In the fictional story of Pinecone Partnership in Chapter 3, it was presumed that this was learned explicitly by everyone in childhood and was generally well understood by the population. It enabled people to resolve conflicts at an early stage. It made co-operation of all sorts much easier. People who are naturally good at it today are generally well liked and are considered to be 'nice'. There is no gene for niceness. It is a basic social skill that can be practised and learned.

11 A peaceful Earth

"Blessed are the peacemakers, for they shall be called the children of God."
Matthew 5:9

"Nothing stands between us and disaster except ourselves. This principle applies to nuclear war as it does to resolving – peacefully, voluntarily, without guns or lawyers – a dispute between neighbors in suburbia over how early it's permissible for a lawnmower to break the morning silence. " Theodore Kheel[111]

This chapter addresses directly the first of the basic eGaian principles from Chapter 6 – Peace. It builds on the communication principles in the last chapter.

The first and most fundamental question is whether peace is possible. Is a well-policed truce the best we can hope for? Is peace even compatible with human nature? Chapter 8 gave examples of cultures in which serious conflict was rare by the standards of Western cultures: the Tahitians, the Yequana of Venezuela, Ladakh, the Fore of New Guinea. But are these exceptional, isolated communities, on the verge of extinction and irrelevant to the wider world?

We have no reason to believe that there has ever been a time when peaceful, collaborative societies were the norm for humanity. If the eGaian social vision does arrive, it will be unprecedented, pushed into existence by the need to overcome the effects of humanity as a global cancer before it is too late.

CONFLICT RESOLUTION

There there has been a lot of work on conflict resolution over the last few decades. Some universities give degrees in it and much research has been done on its roots and causes. Various organisations are now working to

---

[111] Theodore W. Kheel, *The Keys to Conflict Resolution,* Four Walls Eight Windows, New York, 1999, p. xi.

reduce tensions in trouble spots around the world; others are working at the level of the community or the family.

There are some basic principles to be learned from all this work – first, from a few concrete examples.

Navajo peacemaking[112]

The Navajo Nation in the southwestern United States is a self-governing nation that operates within state legal systems, a 'nation within a nation'. It has a process of conflict resolution "taken directly from the traditional methods of dispute resolution used throughout the history of the Navajo people."

"The Navajo philosophy and system of justice focuses on healing both the wrongdoer and all the people that may have been affected – directly and indirectly. Navajo justice does not try to punish anyone. ...The philosophy of Navajo *beehaz' aanii* teaches that everyone and everything is connected, so that the actions of one individual affect many others. Punishment of the individual not only does not help him or her – it also does nothing to help the community."

The Navajo have a formal process that is used whenever it it needed. "...the Peacemaker process transcends the notion of a method of resolving disputes and becomes a powerful tool for healing the inner processes of the individual and the group that contribute to the production of conflict."

The Peacemaker process is "based on the Navajo tradition of 'talking things out'. What Westerners would call a mediator is the *"Naat' aanii"* or "one who speaks wisely and well", who may come out of the Peacemaker Division or may be chosen by the parties involved. He/she is a member of the community, and may be related to the people in conflict or affected by the conflict.

The stages in the peacemaking process are:

---

[112] Jeanmarie Pinto, "Peacemaking as ceremony: the mediation model of the Navajo Nation", *The International Journal of Conflict Management*, 2000, Vol. 11, No. 3, pp. 267-286.

- laying the groundwork
- the opening prayer
- defining the problem – includes allowing "as much time as it may take for the participants to express their anger, frustration, and pain." It also includes reminding them of their connection to the community. "A common admonishment on this theme is to tell an individual that he or she is "acting as if he/she had no relatives".
- creating problem-solving statements
- summarising the session
- commitment and solidarity
- the closing prayer.

Here's an example:

The case of the families who weren't fooled

"A young Navajo woman sued a man for paternity. When they got into court, the woman said, 'He's the father.' The man said, 'No, I'm not.' The judge sent the case to Navajo peacemaker court. The peacemaker sent notice to the man's and woman's families, and they went to the peacemaking. During the peacemaking, they stopped the 'He is/I'm not' talk. The families knew what had been going on all the time and said, 'We're going to talk about what to do about our child.

The young man didn't have a job, and couldn't afford to pay child support. The woman, who lived in a rural area, relied on firewood for heat and cooking fuel. The families agreed that the young man should supply firewood to the woman until he could pay child support.

By involving the child's family, the discussion turned from paternity to a practical discussion of how to solve a problem. There was no question about paternity – and no need for blood tests – because Navajo families know what their children are doing. They also know what is best for their grandchildren ."[113]

---

[113] J.W. Zion, "Stories from the Peacemaker Court", *In Context* (1994, Spring) [www.context.org/ICLIB/IC38/Yazzie.htm], quoted from Jean Pinto, *op. cit.*

There are several important points to draw from this example.

- The people involved in the conflict are part of a community that is important to them. They don't want to be thought of badly or to be excluded from the community. So those principally involved are motivated to try to work towards resolution and the others concerned have a strong influence upon them.

- The principals and the peacemakers share a view that it is important to heal all concerned. The process of peacemaking is one of healing rather than of punishment, reducing the likelihood that an offender will simply withdraw into bitter isolation only to re-offend again later.

- The peacemaking process is essentially a communication process. It allows all concerned to express their views and feelings. They recognise the importance of acknowledging the strong emotions which play a key part in maintaining conflict.

Here's another example of conflict resolution in a culture that is good at it:

Conflict resolution in Ladakh[114]

"A concern not to offend or upset one another is deeply rooted in Ladakhi society; people avoid situations that might lead to friction or conflict. When someone transgresses this unwritten law, …extreme tolerance is the response. And yet, concern for community doesn't have the oppressive effect on the individual that one might have imagined. On the contrary, I am now convinced that being a part of a close-knit community provides a profound sense of security.

In traditional Ladakh, aggression of any sort is exceptionally rare: rare enough to say that it is virtually non-existent."

"One means of ensuring a lack of friction in traditional Ladakh society is something I call the 'spontaneous intermediary'. As soon as any sort of difference arises between two parties, a third party is there to act as arbiter. Whatever the circumstances, whoever is involved, an

---

[114] This example is based upon, and quotes extensively from chapter 2, "We have to live together" in Helena Norberg Hodge, *Ancient Futures, Learning from Ladakh*, Rider, 1991, pp. 45 – 54.

intermediary always seems to be on hand. It happens automatically, without any prompting; the intermediary is not consciously sought and can be anyone who happens to be around; it might be an older sister or a neighbour, or just a passing stranger. I remember watching a five-year-old settling a squabble between two of his friends in this way. They listened to him willingly. The feeling that peace is better than conflict is so deeply ingrained that people turn automatically to a third party."

"Traditional Ladakhi villages are run democratically... disparities in wealth are minimal. ...Many activities that would otherwise require the whole village to sit down and draw up plans – like the painting of the village monastery or arrangements for Losar (New Year) – have been worked out many generations ago and are now done by rotation. Nonetheless, sometimes matters have to be decided on a village level. Larger villages are divided up into *chutsos*, or groups of ten houses, each of which has at least one representative on the village council. This body meets periodically throughout the year and is presided over by the *goba*, or village head.

The *goba* is usually appointed by rotation. If the whole village wants to keep him on, he may hold his position for many years, but otherwise after a year or so, the job will pass on to another householder. One of the *goba's* jobs is to act as adjudicator. Though arguments are unusual, from time to time some differences of opinion arise that need settling."

"Before coming to Ladakh, I had always thought that the best judges were the ones who were in no way connected with the individuals they were judging...but having lived in Ladakh for many years, I have had to change my mind. ...when people settling disputes are intimately acquainted with the parties involved, their judgement is not prejudiced; on the contrary, this very closeness helps them to make fairer and sounder decisions."

"In the traditional Ladakhi village, people have much control over their own lives... rather than being at the mercy of faraway, inflexible bureaucracies and fluctuating markets. ...Ladakhis have been fortunate enough to inherit a society in which the good of the individual is not in

165

conflict with that of the whole community; one person's gain is not another person's loss. Ladakhis are aware that helping others is in their own interest. ...Mutual aid rather than competition shapes the economy. It is, in other words, a synergistic society."

Again, a sense of community and an understanding of its importance are deeply ingrained in the culture, as are mechanisms for dealing with and avoiding conflict in its earliest stages. The 'spontaneous intermediaries' are a particularly important example of this.

The description of the fictional Pinecone Partnership in Chapter 3 included similar features. Everyone is part of various overlapping communities that are important to them and in which they see that their own good is not in conflict with that of others. Dealing with conflicts is seen as an essential part of society and is a basic part of every child's education. In terms of the concepts in the last chapter, conflict resolution works well where the people in conflict have a large shared View, and where part of that View is the importance of conflict resolution.

Conflict escalation among the Jalé of New Guinea [115]

This is a contrasting example – of a culture which doesn't have such extensive conflict resolving institutions. The Jalé people live in the Central Mountains of Western New Guinea (and are not to be confused with the Fore of New Guinea described in Chapter 5). They have a culture without the well-ordered, healing conflict resolution of the examples so far.

"In the absence of political and judicial offices, self-help – often in the form of violent retaliation – is an institutionalised method of conflict resolution when negotiation fails. ...[A] skirmish may mark the beginning of a round of battles and retaliatory raids lasting for weeks, months and even years."

---

[115] This example is based upon Klaus-Friedrich Koch, "Pigs and politics in the New Guinea highlands: Conflict escalation among the Jalé", in Laura Nader and Harry F. Todd, eds., *The Disputing Process–Law in Ten Societies*, Columbia University Press, New York, 1978, pp. 58.

Koch gives an example of a dispute between a father and son that started in 1959. The son returned from a trading trip bringing pandanus kernels that he shared with his father and brothers. The father thought he had been given the less delicious marginal parts of the fruit and an argument followed. The next day, the son was still angry and didn't invite his father to a meal of fruit from a tree the father had given him. The father was so angry at this that he cut down the tree and two others.

The next day the argument erupted again, with more people present. Several arrows were shot, and one hit the son in the thigh. Subsequently, the dispute spread to the villages of the two men and escalated into a war. On the third day of fighting a man was killed. In a later battle a second person was killed and one group of people was driven from their land by the other. An uneasy truce existed for a few years, but in 1964 more fighting broke out.

The Jalé have customs and views of justice which regularly lead to spirals of conflict escalation. When conflict arises there is no attempt by the parties involved or anyone else to help create a shared View. If we were to make a naive judgement of human nature by looking at the Jalé culture we would come to a very different conclusion than if we looked at the Navajo or Ladakhis. But by looking at the different ways in which conflict is handled in these cultures we can see that these result in a different way in which human nature appears to be expressed in different cultures. It is not the case that escalating conflict is a built-in feature of human nature.

Unfortunately, in our modern world, cultures in which conflict resolution is an intimate part of their way of living are quite rare. We are much more like the Jalé than the Ladakhis. We have a very ambiguous view of conflict. At some levels, conflict is institutionalised and encouraged.

An effective modern democracy is expected to have a strong opposition that has a reasonable chance of ousting the party in power. An effective politician is expected to disagree with the opposing party and find fault with them at every opportunity. It is considered reasonable that a law can be passed by a majority of as little as one, that a party with a very small majority should impose its views on a minority that may be nearly as large.

Going for consensus, seeking solutions that genuinely satisfy all sides, is not part of the normal political vocabulary.

In economic terms, conflict in the form of competition is considered the hallmark of effective behaviour. Too little competition is considered undesirable, whether it is because a small number of firms dominate the market, or because a service is provided only by the government. The word 'competitive' is often used as a general-purpose virtue, where what is really meant is efficient and well organised. The underlying assumption is that competition is needed to overcome an inherent conflict of interests between an organisation and those it is meant to serve. Without competition, the organisation would favour its own interests over those of its customers or clients. To a large extent, this is an artefact of our money-based economic system, as chapter 13 will show. The idea of a local organisation run jointly by its staff and customers/clients for the benefit of all is far from the normal reality.

What can we conclude from all of this for the prospects of a peaceful society? Mainly that a peaceful society is not just something that will or won't happen by itself. It can come out of an understanding of conflict, what causes it, and how it can be resolved before it gets out of hand. Conflict can be destructive or it can be extremely creative, depending upon how it is handled. Moreover, a peaceful society cannot be created by superficial action. Peace needs to have its roots deep within a society's political and economic structure.

RESOLVING MAJOR WORLD CONFLICTS

The examples of the Navajo and Ladakh in the previous section indicate some of the necessary conditions for effective conflict resolution:

- that the parties concerned need to be part of a larger community with influence over them and which seeks to keep conflict under control;
- that there are always third parties available to help resolve conflict when it arises.

One of the world's most serious conflicts, between the Israelis and the Palestinians, demonstrates further lessons. This conflict is deeply entrenched and bitter.

The following includes extracts from a book by two people who have been involved at close quarters.[116] Bassam Abu-Sharif is a Palestinian who changed from being an active terrorist/freedom fighter (depending upon your perspective) to leading the internal Palestinian struggle to start the peace process. Uzi Mahnaimi is an Israeli who was an intelligence officer and became a journalist working for a peaceful settlement.

The Israeli-Palestinian conflict

From the Palestinian point of view, the Israelis have expelled most of them from their land, and through their settlements are continuing to do so. The Palestinian's violence is a reaction of despair, which, although arguably self-destructive, they see as desperately defensive.

Bassam: "Until the Zionists came, the Abu-Sharif family had lived in Jerusalem for the better part of 500 years."

From the Israeli point of view, the Arabs are living in land which was historically Jewish. This is the only place where they can be safe from the persecutions they suffered in the past. If the Arabs would only let them be, there would be no problems. But if not, they will show that they cannot just be slaughtered as in the Holocaust. The Israelis retaliate strongly to any attack on them. They see this as entirely defensive.

Uzi: "Gideon [Uzi's father] reached manhood with one very strong conviction: that to survive as a Jew meant learning how to defend yourself – to the death."

The two sides have entirely different world views, in which the other side is demonised. Many, perhaps most, members of each community have almost no contact with the other.

---

[116] Bassam Abu-Sharif and Uzi Mahnaimi, *Tried by Fire, The searing true story of two men at the heart of the struggle between the arabs and the jews*, Little, Brown and Co., 1995.

A Palestinian explains: "I grew up in Gaza hating all Jews, believing that they were bloodsuckers, that they had robbed me of my land, my rights and my freedom and that they killed my fellow men. That was before I met my first Jew."[117]

Uzi: "I knew nothing of the Arabs except that they were all demons. ... Like all Israelis, I had been brought up in the Arab-entirely-wrong/ Israeli-entirely-right school of history. ...The dislike and distrust imparted by this teaching was compounded by the almost total lack of contact between the two communities. ...Most people in Israel know nothing about Arab people, and care less. They have no Arab friends. ...They think themselves superior in every way to the Arabs."

In the January, 2001 election, "The despair and anxiety that possessed the Israeli public – and the total lack of awareness of Palestinian pain and suffering – are what has put Sharon in power".[118] Neither side has any sense of the other as 'ordinary people just trying to get on with their lives', the way they see themselves.

From the point of view of someone sympathetic to both sides, they seem like cousins who have much in common, but have fallen out. There is an ongoing cycle whereby violence on one side creates a violent reaction on the other side that creates another violent reaction, and so on. They react with shock at each new 'outrage' from the other side as more evidence to confirm that the others are truly demons. Yet neither side sees what they are doing as connected to what the other is doing to them. Both sides believe that the other side will respond only to force.

Both sides are traumatised and drained of resources by the war effort and the destruction. The chairman of the Gaza Community Mental Health Programme says that 'martyrs' ('suicide bombers' to the Israelis) almost without exception had suffered severe trauma as children –

[117] quoted by Michael Bond, "This is how we live", *New Scientist*, no. 2342, 11 May 2002, p. 42.

[118] David Grossman writing in *The Guardian, G2*, 8 Feb. 2001, p. 4.

watched their parents killed or humiliated or their homes destroyed – and felt they had to combat their sense of helplessness and victimisation on behalf of their nation.[119]

Very few on either side can really envisage the prospects of true peace. Yet a unified Middle East, with its oil wealth added to Israeli technical and industrial ability could be a world power to reckon with.

Bassam: "Peace should not mean only the end of war. At the same time it must mean the development of joint economic, social and political programmes. Israel could never fully become a part of the Middle East unless and until it made peace with the Palestinians. ...It is through a self-governing Palestinian state... that Israelis will eventually drive to shop in the Souq al-Hamadiyyeh, the magical ancient central market in Damascus."

There is a lot to be learned from this example, which applies to very many other human conflicts. First, there are two communities which are at the same time intimately connected and yet with very limited understanding of each other. Thus each can build up a view of the other's motivations which the other would totally reject. Each community, within itself, is continually regenerating that false view of the other community. Strong emotions stop both sides from even considering the View of the other side.

What of the larger community that (as in the Najaho or Ladakh examples) might have helped resolve the conflict? The world community was polarised by the Cold War until the 1990s and so its efforts at peace-making were largely seen as biased. It is not surprising that what progress has been made has come since the Cold War ended. However, most of the efforts in the peace process seem to be aimed at looking for compromises and then putting intense pressure on both sides to accept them.

From an eGaian perspective, the way to resolve the conflict is not simply to look for some compromise formula. Rather it is to start by breaking down the two communities' false views of each other. Some large-scale cultural

---

[119] Michael Bond, "This is how we live", *op. cit.* p. 43

equivalent of the basic communications cycle described in the last chapter is needed to help people to come to understand each others' Views (ie from each other's perspective). As Uzi Mahnaimi said: "Encountering the Arabs as human beings, I felt my entrenched antipathy to them waning slightly. It was the first stirring of a different kind of consciousness in me... ."[120] He subsequently used his position as a journalist to try to instil some understanding of the Palestinians through information he gained from Bassam Abu-Sharif.

There are various organisations that are taking just such an approach to conflict resolution on an international scale. For example, Search for Common Ground,[121] an NGO with "activities on four continents and offices in nine countries", functions "as social entrepreneurs who design and implement innovative ways to reframe issues and solve problems." Their activities include mediation and facilitation, dialogue workshops, inter-ethnic media projects, conflict-resolution training, arts projects, children's kindergartens, and reduction of stereotypes.

In the Middle East they published "simultaneously in nine newspapers from Istanbul to Tel Aviv to Tunis, with authors' interviews broadcast on BBC Arabic Service... a collection of articles by leading academics, intellectuals, and journalists from seven Arab countries, Israel, and Turkey, presenting a variety of visions of life in the Middle East in the year 2020... For probably the first time, mass audiences throughout the Middle East were exposed, in an uncensored fashion and in their own languages, to what other thinkers in the region envisage and aspire to for their collective future."

Search for Common Ground have done work in Sierra Leone, the US, South Africa and Macedonia, where they say "this collective effort was not sufficient to stop the latest violence. However, we strongly believe that our activities were one factor in preventing the recent fighting from deteriorating into outright civil war, and we remain encouraged that Macedonia has not broken apart."

---

[120] Bassam Abu-Sharif and Uzi Mahnaimi, *op. cit.* p. 140.

[121] http://www.sfcg.org/

One of the projects for Macedonia was a children's TV programme called *Nashe Maalo*, which features a cast of children representing each of the four ethnicities – ethnic Albanian, Macedonian, Roma (Gypsy) and Turkish. It "aims to bridge the cultural divide by offering children a window into each other's lives and by modelling positive strategies for coping with conflict. The program's stories seek to help children appreciate their differences as well as the values they share."

So this organisation's work is based on communication which enables people to understand each other and which explicitly develops skills at conflict resolution. They say, "All our tools are variations of one core method, as described by African National Congress leader Andrew Masondo: 'Understand the differences; act on the commonalities.'"

TECHNIQUES FOR CONFLICT RESOLUTION

> *Conflict is an inescapable part of our daily lives. ...Learning how to deal with conflicts effectively is increasingly an essential life skill needed by every person and every group...[122].*

Unlike the Navajo or the Ladakhis, most modern cultures do not have techniques and principles of conflict resolution at the heart of their culture. However, we do have many specialists with a great deal of skill and experience of handling conflict at many levels – in families and schools, in communities, in international relationships. A peaceful, sustainable eGaian culture will need to learn from these specialists and spread these skills much more widely. A number of these specialists have written popular, well-respected books.

Dudley Weeks has worked on peacemaking and civil rights around the world and in many communities. His book, *The Eight Essential Steps to Conflict Resolution*[123] is an excellent introduction to communication-based conflict resolution. His starting point is that conflict is a natural outgrowth of

---

[122] Dudley Weeks, *The Eight Essential Steps to Conflict Resolution*, Tarcher, Los Angeles, 1992, p. ix.

[123] *ibid.*

diversity among people, not something to be feared and avoided. It can be seen as an opportunity to strengthen a relationship and to learn something new. Of course conflict can be damaging and disruptive and can absorb all of the conflicting party's energies, to the cost of everything else they are trying to do, but that doesn't have to be the case.

Weeks is clear about approaches to conflict resolution that are ineffective. These include 'the conquest approach' in which one party tries to dominate and overcome the other, 'the avoidance approach' in which the parties pretend the conflict doesn't exist, and 'the bargaining approach' in which a temporary solution is found which doesn't satisfy anyone.

The origins of conflict come from diversity. "Diversity is a healthy aspect of human society. Diversity can open up possibilities, challenge us to consider alternatives, and keep us from allowing ourselves to stagnate. We need to celebrate diversity, not fear it or perceive it as a threat."[124] Diversity leads to differing needs, and "discord arises when one or both parties ignore needs... that [the other] define as essential". Sometimes, one party may be ignoring their own needs, which can also allow conflict to fester.

A crucial point here is that needs can be understood only as defined by each party for themselves. "People interpret reality differently. ...people can have different perceptions about how and why the event happened and what the event means. Some of these differing perceptions may actually be... misperceptions; but if the perceiver believes the misperceptions are true, in effect, they become reality to that person."

Power is another "essential ingredient of conflict", and Weeks presents ways to use power constructively. Other essential ingredients are the role of values and principles, and the feelings and emotions of those involved in the conflict.

The basis of Weeks' approach is what he calls 'the conflict partnership process'. It "establishes a foundation on which the people or groups involved in a conflict can transform the adversarial, combative I-versus-you pattern usually found in conflict into a healthy attitude, one in which the

---

[124] *ibid.* p. 33.

tone is: We are working together to improve our relationship and to deal with our differences."

This is consistent with the approach used by Search for Common Ground in the Middle East, or by Bassam and Uzi. They are not just seeking compromises that both sides can accept, but are trying to build mutual understanding, looking towards a vision of a relationship between Israelis and Palestinians in which both sides see the true benefits of peace.

> **You** A nice goal, but not an easy one.

> **Me** I don't think anyone involved in conflict resolution believes it is easy. People can be very attached to their conflicts. Strong emotions block their view of their opponents' needs, and of the possibility of positive outcomes. What is important is to understand what works. Conflict resolution might become easy if we ever get to stage where is has become deeply engrained in our culture, as in Ladakh. That should be our goal.

Weeks' Eight Essential Steps

1. *Create an effective atmosphere* – one that promotes partnership and problem solving.

2. *Clarify perceptions* – both sides need to understand the other's position, even if they don't agree with it. Emotions are legitimate and should be acknowledged. Use 'I – Statements' to tell the other how you feel, rather than 'You – Statements' that blame. Assert your needs without attacking the other.

3. *Focus on individual and shared needs* – Each side should acknowledge the legitimate needs of the other side, as well as those of their own, distinguish between real needs and secondary desires, and identify the other's core goals they can support. Both should realise that they need one another to successfully resolve conflicts.

4. *Build shared positive power* – this promotes building together and strengthening partnerships, rather than imposing the will of one on the other.

5. *Look to the future, then learn from the past* – Images of a positive future relationship can provide motivation to move forward. The past is there to learn from. Forgiveness makes a large difference and may be the key to moving forward.

6. *Generate options* – Often, both sides will be set in entrenched positions, but with a little creativity, many more options will appear.

7. *Develop stepping stones to action* – "Do-ables are specific acts that stand a good chance of success, meet some individual and shared needs, and depend upon positive power, usually shared power, to be implemented".

8. *Make mutual benefit agreements* – Avoid win-lose solutions that damage the long-term relationship. Look for solutions that benefit both sides and that build the relationship.

Another good book is *Getting to Yes, Negotiating an agreement without giving in*, by Roger Fisher, William Ury and Bruce Patton.[125] The authors are directors of the Harvard Negotiation Project, with experience ranging from family settings, labour disputes, ethnic conflicts and international conflicts. Their approach has a similar feel to that of Weeks, but their emphasis is somewhat different. Their overall stance is to avoid bargaining over positions. Always look for the underlying needs of both parties.

The *Getting to Yes* method's four main parts:

1. *Separate the people from the problem.* Issues of personality and especially personality clashes often get intertwined with the problem and need to be separated. Often they result from people's misperceptions of each other, which need to be resolved.

2. *Focus on interests, not positions.* People often stand on entrenched positions that are irreconcilable. However, by looking at the interests they have that underlie their positions, it may be possible to find sympathy and common ground.

3. *Invent options for mutual gain* – very similar to Weeks' 'do-ables'.

---

[125] Arrow Business Books. 1992

4. *Insist on using objective criteria.* The main idea here is to find some criteria other than simply the will of one of the sides. Is there any external basis for deciding what to do that both sides could accept as objective?

> **You** Both of these approaches assume that both sides are reasonable and want to reach a solution. What do you do if one side has much greater power and refuses to negotiate?

> **Me** I don't think either book makes that assumption, although my simplified summaries may give that impression. Certainly it is very much easier if both parties genuinely want a solution. Here is where a larger community helps a lot. Nonetheless, both books suggest ways to help overcome entrenched resistance and power.

SUMMARY ON CONFLICT RESOLUTION

Conflict is a natural part of life and arises from diversity and from differences in perspective. It can be seen as an opportunity to learn from those differences and to find ways of transcending them. The result can be a broader and more adaptive vision.

Conflict resolution is essentially a process of communication. Its essence is that the parties in conflict come to understand each other's positions and feel empathy for each other. This often includes an appreciation of each other's emotional states – anger, fear, pain or whatever. It may include apologies for harm done and forgiveness for injuries received.

Conflict resolution is a process of healing the damage done on all sides, with the result being a restoration of a constructive relationship or the creation of one. Positive steps to build that relationship are an essential part of the process.

When the parties in conflict are part of a larger community with influence upon them, conflicts are much more easily resolved. This is especially so if the community can provide people to mediate and help with the healing process.

This approach to conflict resolution is very different to the mainstream attitudes of most modern societies. Conflict is more often approached through the imposition of force, so that the most powerful prevails, or through punishment and imprisonment. If we are to build a peaceful, sustainable Earth, we will need to let go of our current attitudes towards conflict. An appreciation of the creative power of conflict and a thorough grounding in ways of handling it constructively need to be built into our culture and our educational systems. Any group or organisation which is serious about building a more peaceful, sustainable lifestyle must take the process and techniques of conflict resolution very seriously.

12 A Sustainable Earth

This chapter of the eGaian Guide looks at the second of the three basic eGaian principles – sustainability. What would it mean if humanity were organised so that looking after the health of the whole of the living Earth were one of its primary values? It shows that it is possible that all of humanity could live in modest material comfort, with minimal use of energy and resources, if our economy was organised with that as a goal.

You Didn't we know all that back in the 1970s?

Me Largely, yes. At that time it was all new, and much of it now seems rather naive. We have the benefit of a generation of careful thought and research to turn what were just ideas into mature technologies. And much of the naivety was due to the assumption that sustainability could take place without the sort of fundamental changes in society described in the last two chapters.

The purpose of this chapter is to flesh out what ultimately makes for sustainability. It is pointing towards goals rather than looking at possible first steps, but in so doing will help explore and clarify first steps. Thus it is once again the answer to the 'miracle question'. The miracle question assumes away all the cultural obstacles to sustainability. So it looks at what is desirable for sustainability in physical and biological terms while ignoring constraints due to entrenched beliefs, our current economic system or the ravages of current wars and national or ethnic rivalries.

However, it will not ignore constraints due to the size of the human population. Our population is much too large for us to propose simply that humanity backs off and lets nature regenerate as it did, for example, after each of the last few ice ages. That is why humanity needs to function actively and consciously as a nervous system for the living Earth.

High-level principles for sustainability

There are many measures that are popularly thought of as leading towards sustainability: using less fossil fuels and more renewable energy sources to reduce carbon dioxide emissions; re-cycling glass, paper, cans and plastic; moving towards organic food production rather than intensive, chemical-based industrial agriculture; restricting the effluents which can be dumped into the atmosphere or watercourses; moving towards a more locally-based economy. The list can be extended indefinitely, and every item on it is controversial in some circles, always on economic, but sometimes also on practical grounds.

To clarify the list, there are three high-level principles underpinning sustainability and based on the metaphor of the Earth becoming organism-like.

- *Regeneration and recycling* The most fundamental characteristic of an organism is that throughout the cycle of its life it regenerates itself. It continuously builds and rebuilds, growing new cells as old ones die using the nutrients it gets from its environment. Moreover, the wastes of an organism form the food of some other organism. And then, when it dies, when it can no longer regenerate itself, other organisms use it as food. The result is that the chemicals that make up organisms simply go round and round the biosphere.

- *Stability, resilience and self-repair* Organisms must face the challenges of environments which change and which sometimes damage them. All those which persist over many generations (i.e. are sustainable) can cope with change and repair themselves from injury up to a certain point.

- *Adaptability and creativity* This is simply the response to changing environments over a longer time scale. The organism may evolve to a new form; it may aquire new ways of behaving so that it is better adapted to the new conditions.

So what would it mean for humanity to have these principles applied to the Earth and to themselves as their principal social driving force rather than the pursuit of money?

LAND USE IN AN EGAIAN WORLD

Preserving wilderness

There are parts of the Earth that we think of as natural and unspoiled, meaning that they take their own form, rather than one which is determined by people. Some of these teem with life, like the remaining rainforests, temperate forests, grasslands, and parts of the seas. Others – like deserts, high mountains or the poles – have only scattered life.

The wild areas are biological reservoirs, places where life can live at its most diverse and most stable. These parts of the world can look after themselves and don't need our help, so long as they are big enough and so long as the climate doesn't change too much. They have the properties of regeneration, stability and adaptability described above.

If we suppress the usual assumption that they might offer good opportunities to make money, then the importance to the biological health of the Earth of preserving them becomes obvious and overwhelming. An eGaian world would preserve these as reservoirs, and make them as large as possible. Unfortunately, given the size and continued growth of human population, it is perhaps unlikely that they could be much larger than at present, even under an eGaian human culture.

> **You** When you say 'reservoirs' do you mean that no humans should live within them?
>
> **Me** No, and people do live in them now. I think it desirable that they have small, low-density human populations, living what is essentially a traditional gatherer-hunter lifestyle (but also in communication with the rest of humanity). They would be the caretakers such communities always saw themselves to be. Some would be the continuation of existing indigenous cultures, but treated with a new respect by the rest of humanity. Some entirely new forms of gatherer-hunter cultures might also arise, which people from more settled cultures might move into and out of at different times.

Countryside for food

Outside of wilderness areas, humans and their artefacts to a greater or lesser degree dominate the Earth's surface. Population size means this is likely to continue, but human intervention must be much more natural.

Once we drop the assumption that money flows dominate what we do, our approach to the countryside becomes quite different. The obvious and necessary function of the countryside is to provide food for our huge population. However, the countryside could look very different if our food were seen as our principal connection to the rest of the natural world, and also as the key to our personal health, rather than simply as one more industry or a profitable leisure activity[126].

In the story of Pinecone Partnership (Chapter 3), Elderberry Farm illustrates the changed role of farming. Perhaps its most important characteristic is the provision of food mainly for the local population rather than for global agribusiness.

> **You** Is providing food for world markets such a bad idea?
>
> **Me** I'm afraid it is. I'm not saying that there should be no international trade in food. Far from it. It is just that food should come predominantly from local sources. There is a strong movement for organic food now, but the growing movement for local food, though less known, is at least as important.

The most obvious reason for food provision to be primarily local is freshness – for flavour, preservation of nutrients and health. It also removes the need for so much processing and packaging. Locally produced meat reduces some animal welfare issues. And for reviving the connection between people and the natural world there is nothing better than a connection with the food they eat.

Producing food for the global market shares many of the difficulties of globalisation of all products. For a start, there is a tremendous amount of

---

[126] Colin Tudge, <u>Feeding People is Easy</u>, Pari Publishing, 2007.

extra transport. A typical plate of food in the US today has accumulated some 1,500 miles from source to table. In 1997 food transport was 20% of the total for US commodity transport. And that is just internal transport of food, not including imports, infrastructure costs or car trips to the supermarket.

It is not a matter of giving the consumer more choice. Equivalent products go both ways. For example, the UK imported 114,000 tonnes of milk in 1996 and exported 119,000 tonnes. A supermarket may supply half a dozen varieties of apples from around the world. Yet it probably offers no interesting local varieties because they aren't as suited to industrial scales of growing and handling.[127]

"Americans import Danish sugar cookies, and Danes import American sugar cookies. Exchanging recipes would surely be more efficient."[128]

Food provision can be considered in terms of the high-level principles for sustainability listed above. First, regeneration and recycling: Elderberry Farm is a mixed organic farm, which includes crops, animals, woodland and mixed grassland. It is a recycling centre for wastes, and supplies its own energy. It doesn't need external inputs such as fertilisers and pesticides or fossil fuels for its tractors. It is designed to fit into natural biological cycles.

The second principle is stability, resilience and self-repair. For a start, if food is produced locally, adapted to the local area, it is not susceptible to the ups and downs of the world commercial market. As to the nature of the farming, Elderberry Farm has a lot of perennial crops plus wild and semi-wild animals. That means it is a lot closer to self-regulation than conventional farms today. Because of its variety of species, it is not subject to the kind of diseases that can spread through monocultural agricultural systems. It uses a variety of biological controls for pests and diseases.

---

[127] Helena Norberg Hodge, Todd Merrifield and Steven Gorelick, *Bringing the food economy home,* International Society for Ecology and Culture, October, 2000, p. 11.

[128] Herman Daly, "The perils of free trade", *Scientific American,* vol. 269, no. 5, Nov. 1993, p. 51.

"In some cases, the farm itself mimics the wilderness, as in the traditional forest gardens of the Tamil Nadu highlands in southern India. These gardens produced a fantastic array of fruits, nuts, berries, roots and edible leaves, while relying on the forest's indigenous species – including micro-organisms, insects, wild animals and 'non-productive' plants – to maintain the garden's balance and health."[129]

Studies show that current farming practices are a principal cause of the loss of bio-diversity in the world today. This reduces the stability of the biosphere. It is the combination of mixed, pseudo-natural farms and the preservation of the remaining wilderness areas that are the main eGaian means of stopping this loss.

Probably the most important effect of sustainable agriculture would be to halt the decline in soil fertility and the loss of topsoil. This is one of the most dangerous by-products of industrial agriculture. For example, it is estimated that five pounds of topsoil are lost for every pound of grain harvested in Iowa.[130]

> **You** But surely this use of perennial crops, organic agriculture, and wild animals is much less productive than today's intensive farms. It sounds like a nice idea, but you have said we are going to have to feed nearly twice as many people as we do today.

> **Me** The idea that sustainable agricultural systems are inherently lower yielding doesn't seem to be borne out by research. Much of today's mainstream food research, such as most of that into genetically modified crops is motivated by a desire to improve money flows in agriculture.

Jules Pretty writes about sustainable agriculture[131] characterised by:

---

[129] Helena Norberg Hodge, et. al. *op. cit.* p. 17.

[130] *ibid*, p. 20

[131] Jules N. Pretty, *Regenerating Agriculture*, Earthscan, London, 1995.

- use of natural processes such as nutrient cycling, nitrogen fixation and pest-predator relationships;
- reduction in external inputs;
- more equitable access to productive resources;
- use of the biological and genetic potential of plants and animals;
- use of local knowledge and practices;
- better match of cropping patterns to climate and landscape;
- integrated farm management to conserve soil, water, energy and biological resources.

This is all very much consistent with the Elderberry Farm practices. Pretty describes the effect of sustainable agriculture in three different areas.

- In industrialised countries, about 1.2 billion people rely on agriculture with large external inputs (fertiliser, pesticides, transport, etc). Sustainable methods would lower yields by perhaps 10-20%, but remove the need for the external inputs. These are areas where the population is not growing and which currently have food surpluses.
- In the Third World, there are roughly 2.5 billion people whose food relies on 'green revolution' type farming methods – a few high yielding varieties which need a lot of water, fertiliser and pesticides. There, sustainable agricultural methods could match current productivity.
- In the poorest countries, there are about 1.2 billion people who use traditional agricultural methods, often on the poorest land (since the better land has gone into the global market). There, using the modern sustainable approaches Pretty describes could double or treble output.

> **You** Still, on that analysis, feeding the Earth's future human population doesn't look too easy.
>
> **Me** Not easy but not out of the question, which is how I see the whole transition to an eGaian world.

And what about the third high-level principle for sustainability – adaptability and creativity? Elderberry Farm used several networks to ensure that its practices were up-to-date and appropriate. It was monitored by its staff and linked into the scientific community to ensure that its results and its methods were the best practice available. And in a different sense of creativity, it was laid out with a strong sense of the aesthetic, so that it would have a visual appeal to the local population.

It is clear from the Elderberry Farm story that a lot of creativity needs to be put into the nature of food production if we are to move towards sustainability in that aspect of our lives. The growing popularity of organic food is only a small beginning. Supermarket organic food may not be grown with fertilisers and pesticides but it is still industrially grown and distributed food.

Urban and industrial areas

An eGaian world would still have urban and industrial areas, but they too would be changed significantly, towards a more organic form following the high-level principles for sustainability.

> **You** So you don't envisage a totally back-to-nature world then?

> **Me** No, that is not my vision. I grew up in a large city and understand their appeal as cultural and organisational centres. But I imagine that cities could actually be changed sufficiently so that they would fit in with an eGaian world.

Their food would come predominantly from the surrounding countryside for all the reasons given above. Some food would come from more distant places to provide interest and variety in people's diets, rather than because of market opportunities. In addition there would be a major expansion of urban garden-parks, to produce some of the local food, and – probably in some cities – the development of large market gardens within the city boundaries, as was the tradition in Beijing, for example.

Urban and industrial areas require enormous inputs of materials and finished goods, and large exports of the same. They have very large inputs of energy as electricity and as fuels and large outputs of waste heat and combustion products such as carbon dioxide and more toxic emissions. They have large outputs of wastes of all kinds. The following sections indicate how production and energy might be developed sustainably.

MAKING THINGS SUSTAINABLY

It should be clear by now that the eGaian image is in no sense a return to a low-tech, primarily rural pre-industrial world. But very dramatic changes in the way we make and distribute things will be needed to move towards sustainability. Over the past few decades a tremendous amount of research and thinking has been devoted to this subject. The eGaian image builds on this and projects it into the future, looking at what is desirable in physical, biological and social terms freed from the constraints of the present economic system.

Several parts of the Pinecone Partnership story illustrate this approach to sustainability, most especially the Pinecone Plastics factory, but also Apple Transport and the Transport Users Co-op, and the Pinecone Communications Workshop. As with food production, most products are made locally, customised to suit local needs. However, this is not done because of an ideological commitment to local self-sufficiency, but for practical reasons. If there are some products for which only a few high-volume production factories make more sense (for example, computer chips as opposed to computer assembly) than that is the strategy to adopt.

Local production dramatically reduces transport and the energy needed for it. It means that goods are designed for the needs of local people, not for some global mass market. The eGaian goal is largely local production but with global connections for ideas, advice and support.

The Pinecone Plastics factory illustrates and extends what is best in current environmental thinking about product design and manufacturing. The raw materials for its plastics come from local renewable resources (chemicals derived from wood and other organic materials). Its plastics are designed to be recycled and re-manufactured into other products when they reach the end of their life. This is a direct application of the first of the high level sustainability principles – regeneration and recycling.

Similarly, Apple Transport and Pinecone Communications products are designed so that their useful life can be extended by repair and updating of parts, with obsolete parts recycled and re-used.

These strategies reduce the amount of production needed, so reducing water and energy needs, raw materials and waste materials. As a result, they also reduce the workload of the organisations, giving their employees an easier life. Of course in our present economic system this would be a disaster for the three firms in question, as they would prefer to keep their production as high as possible to increase their income. Local production of long-life, customised recyclable products is good for the environment and all the people concerned but bad for an economy that is driven by producers' needs.

> **You** I must admit that this goes way beyond the kind of recycling of bottles, cans and paper I am used to.

> **Me** Yes, I hope it is clear why that is really just a token effort.

The strategies illustrated in Pinecone Partnership are part of what is now called 'ecodesign' or 'life cycle design' that aims:

> "to reduce and balance the adverse impact of manufactured products on the environment by considering the product's whole life cycle – from raw materials acquisition, through manufacture, distribution and use, to reuse, recycling and final disposal."[132]

Strategies include:

1. "the selection of low-impact (e.g. renewable) materials;

2. reducing the weight or volume of materials in the product;

3. using cleaner (e.g. less wasteful, polluting) techniques for product manufacture;

4. reduction of environmental impacts arising from the packaging and distribution of the product;

5. reduction of environmental impacts arising from the use (e.g. energy consumption) and maintenance of the product;

6. optimising the life of the product (e.g. by creating durable 'classic' designs);

---

[132] Robin Roy, "Sustainable product-service systems", *Futures* 32 (2000), p. 290.

7. reuse, remanufacture, recycling or disposal at the end of the product's life."[133]

Moving towards a sustainable world will involve reducing energy, water and resource flows, as well as waste and pollution generated, by anything from four to 20 times,[134] particularly in the more affluent industrialised countries. The strategies of ecodesign described above are only a part of what is needed. Roy talks about them as part of 'sustainable product-service systems'[135], which also include:

- systems designed to satisfy needs rather than provide products. For example, the Transport Users Co-op in Pinecone Partnership helps people with their transport rather than providing them with their own cars. Providing home insulation to keep people's homes warm rather than increasing the supply of gas or oil for heating is another example.

- sharing of services. Again, in the Transport Users Co-op, vehicles are shared so fewer are needed.

- product life extension services. This is very much in the model of Apple Transport or the Pinecone Communications Workshop, in which the organisation takes complete responsibility for the product (car or computer), from manufacture to maintenance to recycling.

- demand side management. Instead of taking the demand for something for granted and supplying it, a partnership between producer and consumer enables demand to be altered to suit conditions. For example, the Pinecone Plastics factory used renewable energy sources and adjusted its output somewhat according to how much energy was available. The Transport Users Co-op arranges shared transport for people so that for minor changes in their preferred travel plans large savings are made by sharing transport.

---

[133] *ibid.* p. 290-291.

[134] Ernst von Weisacker, Amory Lovins, A, and L. Hunter Lovins, *Factor Four. Doubling wealth, halving resource use*, Earthscan, London 1997.

[135] Robin Roy, *op. cit.*

All of these strategies for improving the sustainability of producing and using things are much easier and more obviously desirable in a society which is organised for co-operation (as is assumed in the Pinecone Network) than in our current competitive market economy.

SUSTAINABLE ENERGY USE

This is probably the highest profile issue in current debates on sustainability because the carbon dioxide released by burning coal, oil and gas is the principal cause of global warming. However there are many other problems with our present use of energy,[136] including acid rain, oil pollution of the seas, radioactive wastes and the decommissioning of nuclear energy plants. Moreover, the concentration of fuel reserves in a small number of countries (especially in the Middle East) adds enormously to political tensions around the world.

In an eGaian future these problems would be eliminated through a variety of strategies. The most important of these is the reduction in the need for energy (but with only minor reductions in people's comfort). Much of this has already been covered in the preceding sections. Local production of food and other goods plus the greatly increased use of shared transport hugely reduces the need for fuels for transport.

Much of the rest of the ecodesign and sustainable product-service systems also acts to reduce the need for energy. Some do this directly, as in more highly insulated buildings and other energy-saving techniques (low-energy light bulbs, better controls for heating systems, etc). Others do it indirectly. If the lifetime of products are extended through design, re-use and recycling of parts, much less need to be produced, saving the energy of production. Less raw materials need to be mined, quarried and transported, removing the energy needed for that. If things are shared and used more efficiently then less of them need to be produced, saving that energy.

---

[136] Gary Alexander, "Overview: the context of renewable energy technologies", in Godfrey Boyle, *Renewable Energy, Power for a Sustainable Future,* Oxford University Press, 1996, pp. 19-26.

There are also other, wider ways to reduce energy needs, such as the re-use of energy flows. Collecting the waste heat from electricity generation and using it for heating buildings is one example.

From research done in the recent past, it looks likely that we could "accomplish everything we do today as well as now or better, with only one-quarter of the energy and materials we presently use."[137] In an eGaian future, when ecodesign would be central to social goals and thus much more highly developed, our needs for energy and materials could probably be reduced much further. (The changes resulting from the effort that has gone into improving computers and mobile phones are clues to what might be achieved.) For example, in an eGaian future there might be virtually no need to mine for more metals. The recycling and re-use of metal parts combined with mining our old rubbish might be sufficient.

> **You** I thought this section was going to be about renewable energy, like wind power and all that?
>
> **Me** Yes, I'm just about to get to that. This discussion of reducing our needs was necessary first.

Traditional discussions about energy concentrate on supplies – like how many more power stations would be needed. They assume continuing economic growth and energy needs and conclude that so much energy is needed that renewable sources could supply only a fraction of them. But, once the possibilities of reducing energy needs are exploited, then there is no longer a problem in meeting all of humanity's energy needs purely from renewable sources.

For example, a United Nations study in 1992 concluded that "by the middle of the twenty-first century, renewable sources of energy could account for three-fifths of the world's electricity market and two-fifths of the market for fuels used directly."[138] This study assumed substantial

---

[137] von Weisacker, et. al, *op. cit.*, p. xxi.

[138] T.B. Johansson, H. Kelly, A.K. Reddy, , and R.H. Williams, (eds) *Renewable Energy: Sources for Fuel and Electricity*, Island Press, Washington, D.C., 1993.

economic growth and increased world energy consumption. With eGaian assumptions, there would easily be enough for all the world's energy requirements.

The Pinecone Partnership story gives a flavour of how this would work. There are renewable sources of energy in many places. Elderberry Farm has some large wind turbines to produce electricity. It also uses a certain amount of coppiced wood as fuel and takes in wastes that are processed into liquid and gaseous fuels. Pinecone Plastics and many other buildings have solar panels that produce electricity and heat.

The basic principle is to use whatever diverse forms of energy are available, whether direct solar energy, wind energy, energy from rivers and streams, biomass energy from wood and wastes, and in coastal areas wave and tidal energy and offshore wind energy.

> **You** Does this mean that there would no longer be those horrible lines of electricity pylons marching across the countryside?
>
> **Me** I'm afraid it doesn't, although they might be smaller.

The principle here, as with food and goods, is that energy production is basically local, but connected globally. With energy supplies this is particularly important. There are still likely to be some larger sources of energy, such as the offshore wind and wave sources and some hydroelectric schemes where the energy needs to be distributed over an area. Also, renewable energy sources are very variable. By connecting them in a grid you average them out. A high wind in one place might provide more energy than is needed there, but will supply a place where there is no wind at that moment. At times when the variable sources are below requirements, the supply can be topped up with generators running on gas or liquid fuels (renewably made, of course). In a similar way, there could be gas distribution networks, as there are now, but supplying gas from a large number of local gasifiers fed using wood and wastes.

At present, transport is a major user of fuels. In an eGaia world, this would be much reduced because local production means much less need for transport fuels.

In addition, there would be a much greater use of bicycles, for those people who are fit enough. There are further substantial synergies from the use of electric vehicles of all sorts. Using electricity for transport is much more efficient than burning fuels. It would require an infrastructure of charging stations, which is now growing. These batteries under charge could provide an extra function as storage to balance the variability of renewable energy sources.

This approach to supplying energy locally but linked into a network follows the first two high-level principles. Energy is just one more part of the local regeneration and recycling system. Local but linked energy sources provide much more resilience than do large, centralised power stations. And of course there is no longer the problem of fluctuating fuel prices due to political events halfway around the world.

TOWARDS A SUSTAINABLE EARTH

By looking at the use of land, especially for food, and at sustainable methods of producing goods and energy, it should be clear that sustainability is possible in physical and biological terms without the need to revert to a pre-industrial lifestyle. The obstacles to implementing these strategies are organisational and economic, not physical and biological. Such obstacles are not inevitable, although they are major. They are of the form "changing the side of the road on which you drive" rather than "changing the law of gravity".

We don't need industrial agriculture to feed a growing world population. On the contrary, industrial agriculture is a major contributor to poverty and to the destruction of the environment. We need largely local organic food production that mimics natural ecosystems, but linked in a global human food web.

We don't need globalised production and distribution of goods to make the world prosperous. It serves the financial needs of global corporations but not the needs of the environment. It does a bad job for most of the human population. We need largely local production, tailored to local needs, designed for maximum re-use and minimum waste, but linked to a global information and support network.

We don't need more nuclear power stations, oil tankers or fracking to keep the lights on and to keep us supplied with goods. That serves the needs of those industries while creating pollution and destabilising the climate. We need largely local energy sources, exploiting whatever forms of renewable energy are available locally, but linked into regional grids.

The physical and biological side of sustainability is much easier to envisage than the social and economic. Growing a peaceful, collaborative world is the hardest part. If we can begin to get that established then sustainability will fall into place easily. And the possible steps in that direction are the subject of the next few chapters.

13 A co-operative economy

If there is to be any chance of creating a peaceful, sustainable world, its economy will have to be very different from at present. It will need to provide a modest level of material comfort for all of the world's population, but with minimal use of energy and resources. The previous chapter showed how the principles that were implicit in the fictional *Taste of an eGaian Future* in Chapter 3, could accomplish that in physical terms. This chapter looks at the social side.

It describes a co-operative economy, building on the principles in the chapters on relationships and conflict resolution. This means much more than, for example, workers co-operatives competing against each other in the market. It means co-operation on all scales from local to global, as a single, co-ordinated global economy. This chapter looks at the organising principles of how it could be done, then gives the reasons why this is needed. Finally, Part 4 of the book tackles the key question: Could we get to a vision such as this or is it just a hopeless dream?

> **You** I can see that there is a lot wrong with our economy, but what is wrong with having markets? Surely central planning is worse? And why co-operative on all scales?

> **Me** I think this is the area where I go further than many others who are trying to re-think the global economy, so I'll try to be very clear about it. I introduced this in *Chapter 3 A taste of an eGaian future*, where there certainly was no central planning, but there was global co-ordination. It is a myth that the only alternative to the market is central planning (which I agree is worse in principle because the planners, even if they are benevolent, cannot take into account the variety of local needs).

The appeal of the market is its apparent freedom, the apparent autonomy of its components. Individuals and organisations can operate as they see best, as understood from their own perspectives.

The eGaian version retains that freedom and autonomy. It does not impose a central control, but rather changes the relationship from competition to co-operation. It is self-organised free exchange based upon individuals and organisations appreciating the advantages of co-operation and mutual support.

It has local businesses and co-operatives each with their own specialities and regular customers, so they are not in competition with each other. They can then work together in an organised fashion to make sure each is working in the most efficient manner, is environmentally sound, and is satisfying its customers as best it can. This co-ordination takes place at many scales: the very local, the regional, and even globally where appropriate.

It is very hard to see through our modern economy to the roots of its problems, because we are so immersed in it and it has grown to its present form over such a long period of time. Some of the more popular proposed solutions do not get to those roots. For example, there are proposals for changing the tax system to include environmental costs.[139] Another alternative is government regulation: "It is regulation rather than taxation that more efficiently improves the market."[140] These proposals are unlikely to be implemented in a strong enough form to make much difference – witness the difficulties getting approval of the Kyoto agreement limiting carbon dioxide emissions. Moreover, if they were implemented, they wouldn't solve the problems to anything like the extent their proponents believe, as will be clear by the end of this chapter.

---

[139] For example, D. Pearce, "The practical implications of sustainable development", in P. Ekins & M. Max-Neef, *op. cit.*, pp. 403-411, or Ernst vonWeizsacker, Amory B. Lovins, L. Hunter Lovins, *Factor Four, Doubling Wealth, Halving Resource Use*, Earthscan, London, 1997.

[140] T. Jackson and M. Jacobs, "Carbon taxes and the assumptions of environmental economics", in T. Barker (ed.), *Green Futures for Economics*, Cambridge Econometrics, Cambridge, 1991,p. 62.

ORGANISING PRINCIPLES FOR A CO-OPERATIVE ECONOMY

We are all familiar with the way a competitive market economy works, as in one form or another it has been around since the earliest civilisations. At the same time, we have all experienced co-operative communities to some degree or other. As we saw in *Chapter 8 The Co-operative Ape*, they were what forged human evolution, and so are our birthright. How then, can we put the best of both together to form the basis of a mature human civilisation that works for people and planet? That is the task of this section.

To start with, there is very much in the modern economy that could and should continue. Most production, distribution and services would be done largely on a professional, well-organised basis. This is not an 'everybody bakes their own bread, makes their own sandals, builds their own house' vision, although there might be more people doing things for themselves and a higher proportion than at present done on a craft basis rather than on a mass-production basis. The skill and efficiency that comes when things are done by people with training, experience and the right tools will be as vital in the future as it is now.

The modern economy is made up of organisations of different sizes, from local firms to large corporations with many branches, perhaps world wide. An eGaian co-operative economy would also have a diversity of organisations but they would be co-operating, not competing.

If this vast ecosystem of organisations comes to function efficiently and effectively in collaboration, with goals the wellbeing of all the world's people and the health of the environment, then the metaphor of the Earth functioning as an organism with humanity as its nervous system will fit.

I see four major principles as useful:

1. *Information*: Many forms of information – about what is needed and wanted, about quality, customer experience, best practice, about real, social and environmental costs – guide what people and enterprises do, replacing much of the function of money and reducing its dysfunctionality.

2. *Niches*: Each productive enterprise has its own unique and distinctive specialisation, its 'niche': whom do they usually serve? and who supplies them? This enables them to co-operate with similar enterprises instead of compete with them.

3. *Autonomy with co-ordination at a range of scales*: Each productive enterprise has as much autonomy as possible, while being immersed in a supportive relationship with other enterprises, and the larger economy. This gives them the advantages of scale we now see with multinationals while serving wellbeing for people and planet.

4. *Money systems that support exchange without dominating:* Where there is residual use of money, it comes into and out of existence as needed to facilitate exchange.

> **You** So you will have some use for money in your co-operative economy?

> **Me** I suspect that as a co-operative economy develops, people will begin to find that money gets in the way, and that it will be used less as the other systems take over. But a moneyless economy would be quite a late stage. In the early stages of a transition, I think it is sufficient that people understand the problems money causes and begin to find ways around them. There will be various new financial institutions (like community banks and loan funds or peer-to-peer lending) and new forms of money (local and electronic currencies) that will grow up as needed.

Information

For a co-operative economy to develop with all the complexity of modern societies, the crucial ingredient will be its information systems, very likely as an extension of today's online social networks. Money now provides the information that is the principle determinant of what gets done and who gets what in the economy. Today, whether it is buying food in a shop, or deciding whether to build a new airport, the financial cost is crucial. Potential financial costs, often expressed as business plans, are a key planning and decision-making tool.

The concept of 'cost' meaning the implications of doing something, is very important, but unfortunately, the cost in money is often a very poor guide, and distorts the decision. For a start, there is a large arbitrary and changing element, such as the exchange rate between currencies. And while the cost of living is low, for example, in China or India, low wages mean it makes sense in financial terms to do your manufacturing there. Wages are very different in different places, largely because of power relationships. It is not more efficient in some physical sense or more sensible in some social sense to manufacture in India and China and ship products around the world. It is an artefact of our money system.

At a personal level, people need to know the effects of their consumption. The idea of an 'environmental footprint' is a simplified version of the concept of 'real cost' which is the full implications of consuming something. . The concept of 'real cost' is much richer than monetary cost. It can be divided into two parts:

- *The physical and biological impact of the object* What materials are required to create it and what is their impact upon the natural world (e.g.. mining, oil wells, forestry?) How much energy and how much water are required in its manufacturing and transport? What are the environmental effects of manufacturing and transporting it? What is required to dispose of it when its useful life is over?

- *The human impact of producing the object* How many hours of effort did it take to produce and distribute it? Under what social conditions was it produced?

At present we have no clear understanding of how to present real costs so that consumers can make informed choices, but there are beginnings. For many products in the West, labels are required to include lists of ingredients. There are the beginnings of rating systems, as an energy ratings for large appliances and houses.

Green consumer magazines such as *Ethical Consumer*[141] evaluate products on a range of issues, including environmental considerations, animal welfare,

---

[141] http://www.ethicalconsumer.org/

effects on people, and 'extras' such as political donations and genetic engineering. There is a rating for several sub-categories of each issue. The point is to enable consumers to decide to purchase or not on much richer information than monetary cost or the one-sided information the producer provides. In contrast to this, the monetary cost of a product leaves out much of what makes up the real cost, especially environmental impact and the social conditions of labour, and reduces the rest to a single number.

Then there is quality. It is sometimes true that a more expensive product is of higher quality than a cheaper one, but often pricing reflects a marketing decision, not costs or quality or level of service. Online sales, starting with eBay, pioneered the idea of customer ratings and reviews, and this is now very common. Before buying most consumer goods, one can find out what other users and professional critics thought about them.

This can be taken very much further if there is are serious moves towards a co-operative economy. Social networks, which already link people and local businesses, could be extended to include a co-operative exchange platform. This could include ratings and reviews by customers so that the public reputation of everyone and all businesses is on display.

It could include a new 'real cost' statement, and extension of the energy ratings some appliances now must show.

You So are you envisaging a much richer kind of price tag?

Me Yes, exactly. As well as money cost, we could have a set of symbols that indicate energy, resource use, hours of labour, and labour conditions. The money cost, a single number, cannot reflect the full richness of the concept of real cost.

These information systems can become the principal social controls, and enable money to be gradually phased out.

Most of the information systems described above can be introduced independently of any other changes in the economy, without requiring any radical changes. They can gently move us towards an economy where quality and service drive businesses, rather than financial gain.

Niches

Today most parts of the economy are dominated by a small number of huge, global corporations – a small number of oil companies, drug companies, car manufacturers, banks, etc. Within their sector they compete fiercely for market share. That competition takes up a lot of their attention, and it is fear of loss of market share that is supposed to ensure that they serve their markets well and keep up quality standards. That is also why most governments have introduced laws to ensure that companies do compete, rather than collude at the expense of the consumer.

> **You**: Surely, if you end competition, won't your future companies be able to ignore what their customers want, as we have seen in planned economies and government-run services?

> **Me**: That's a major reason why I am not proposing planned economies or government run services. If a business is driven by profit, not service, that creates an in-built conflict between its interests and that of its customers. If instead, its goals are to provide wellbeing, and if it has information systems that display its quality and reputation, that conflict is removed.

When businesses are in competition for the same customers, there is a tendency for their products to converge to a common popular point (look how similar different makes of car have become), rather than serve a distinct market well. They all produce similar products, but with different ranges serving different parts of the market.

On the other hand, if a business has its own distinctive niche, which may be specialised offerings, or simply a location near its customers, or even a set of loyal, well-satisfied customers, it is no longer in competition with similar businesses. It becomes free to serve those customers specific needs, and to collaborate with similar businesses for mutual benefit.

In the fictional story about Pinecone Partnership, Apple Transport served its regular customers, whose needs it came to know in depth. Most customers stayed with it because they appreciated the value of a relationship in which their needs were understood. They were free to change garages, and sometimes did for some reason or other. Apple

Transport's job was then to learn whatever lesson they could from that change.

Autonomy with co-ordination

When people think of very large scale organisations, they mostly think in terms of hierarchies. Head office is in overall control, determining what the regional offices do, who in turn control local branches. At all levels it is the higher level that controls the lower. This model has grown from experience with armies, and is the norm in large-scale businesses.

Alternatives where there is a lot of local autonomy, but with co-ordination at regional and larger scales are less widespread, but various models have been tried. The approach described here is based primarily on the work of a 20th century systems thinker named Stafford Beer, and is called Viable Systems Theory.[142] It has been taken up by various management consultants and put into practice in a range of organisations.

Essentially the idea is to put as much responsibility and decision making as possible at the lowest levels of an organisation, to the people actually doing the work, but with co-ordination to ensure that they are taking into account the needs of their customers or clients, suppliers, similar local groups, and the wider environment. The same approach is used at different scales, possibly within an organisation if it is big enough – locally, regionally, nationally, and globally as appropriate. The key words are 'autonomy' and 'synergy'.

For example, in the Pinecone Partnership story, all the businesses such as the farms and transport groups would have autonomy, but also have extensive feedback from their customers, suppliers and peer review so they knew how well they were doing, and were making use of best practice. Where one had specialist equipment or skills, others might refer customers to them. If there were difficulties, such as illness, they would cover for each other.

------

[142] The most readable account of this I have found is <u>The Viable Systems Model, a guide for co-operatives and federations</u> by Jon Walker

At each level there are the groups or organisations that do the actual work, and also a co-ordinating group (the 'meta-system' in viable systems terms), with members generally drawn from the primary groups, whose function is to help them work together effectively. The people handling the co-ordination are not the 'bosses' who can tell the others what to do. Their function is to look at four areas:

1. Stability: Each group is monitored to see whether it is functioning well, and support is offered where needed. The information systems need to look at key performance indicators to help with this. In particular, there need to be organised systems for handling conflicts between people constructively, as these arise routinely. and a culture in which people who find themselves in conflict with others feel pressure from their community to find a way to resolve it constructively.

2. Optimisation: Here the key is synergy. Are there ways in which different groups can support each other? Make best use of the strengths of each? Keep their respective niches clear? How can the collective resources be allocated for these purposes?

3. Adaptation: planning that takes into account the external environment. Developments within and outside of the group of organisations must be monitored, and form the ground of planning activities.

4. Policy and identity: Here the co-ordinating group works with all concerned, to ensure that there is agreement on fundamental principles and policies, so all are working to the same goals.

This combination of autonomy with co-ordination, at all scales large and small, builds heavily on the information systems, ensures that the niches are clear, and enables the whole group to function as an effective mutual support system, optimising wellbeing for people and the natural world.

Money systems that support exchange without dominating

In the Pinecone Partnership story there were three different types of 'money' system, used at different scales. These are only some of the possibilities, and there is no way of knowing what will be appropriate for a given community. What is important is:

- That any money systems don't dominate so that the goals and purpose of an enterprise can be to serve the wellbeing of people and planet rather than to make money.
- That money systems function to enable people to exchange with each other as needed. That is, money should be freely available, not in short supply.

The local system of exchange within Pinecone Partnership was a form of 'gift economy' or generalised reciprocity, as described in Chapter 8. People give to and receive from each other, within the closed group of the Partnership, but without a specific return on each transaction. There are records of what is exchanged so people know how much everyone is giving and getting. The records include ratings, so people have to be careful of their reputation. There is a lot of feedback about what is wanted and needed.

Clearly, in this form of exchange, money doesn't dominate, and people can exchange freely, without any constraints due to lack of money.

> **You** I would say that is exchange without money.

> **Me** Yes, it isn't really money as we think of it, but there is the use of information systems that replace its function.

There were two other forms of money in Pinecone Partnership, which illustrate some of the possibilities for money that supports exchange within a community without dominating.

The Regional Bank issued a form of local currency. There are now very many different alternatives to national currencies in use around the world, sometimes called local, community or complementary currencies[143]. The currency offered by the Regional Bank, the Walnut, as with most current complementary currencies was not 'legal tender', that is no-one is obliged to accept it. Its function is to enable people who are members of its community to exchange with each other, where there isn't a close enough relationship of trust to allow use of generalised reciprocity.

---

[143] See for example the wikipedia article on complementary currencies and its references for more information.

There are various ways in which the amount of money in a complementary currency can be regulated. One of the most common is a 'mutual credit' system, where when one person pays another, the sum paid is added to the account of one and subtracted from the other, even if it means one persons' account becoming negative. In this way money is created at each transaction and disappears when it is given to a person whose balance is negative. Thus the quantity of money is self-regulating, and is never in short supply. There is usually no interest charged, but there are overall fees to cover the running costs of the system.

The third form of money in the Pinecone Partnership story was the 'Eco' which was a new global currency. There have been proposals for such universal currencies[144]. In principle it would be available to all people, and probably would be a mutual credit currency, so its supply automatically adjusts to need. Unlike modern national currencies, it would not be created through loans at interest. Instead, loans would be interest free but there would be charges to cover the overheads of the currency. Thus, unlike conventional currencies, it would not create a built-in need for economic growth to enable people to repay the interest.

WHY IS A CO-OPERATIVE ECONOMY NECESSARY?

> **Me** I hope you now have some sense of how a co-operative economy might function, and how it enables exchange that is driven by wellbeing and service rather than by a desire to make money. We are now in a position to look at why this is so vital.

Two of the main characteristics of our current market economy are that

- it is inherently unstable. There is the 'business cycle' with its recessions alternating with periods of expansion, and widespread insecurity of businesses always fighting for survival and individuals worried about losing their jobs.

---

[144] For example, the Terra, proposed by Bernard Lietar.

- it is hugely inefficient. Vast amounts of productive effort go into conflict and competition, and into activities that are not socially useful or are destructive, as described in the chapter on the global cancer. In a future in which energy and resources are scarce, we cannot afford this.

A co-operative economy is inherently stable and resilient

An economy that is co-operative at all scales, as described in the section on autonomy with co-ordination, is set up to be stable, self-correcting and resilient. That is one of the main and explicit purposes of the 'viable systems' approach described there. Two of the functions of the co-ordinating groups at all scales are to monitor stability and conflicts and correct them, and to adapt to a changing environment.

So, for example, a company that manufactures products can raise or lower their output depending upon need, can share resources, including trained employees, with neighbouring firms so each helps the other when needed.

A locally-based but globally co-ordinated economy is one in which every organisation has the autonomy to best serve its clients and suppliers, while receiving support to adapt to changes in the environment. All see themselves as part of the larger whole and work together for its best interests.

In contrast to that, in the present economy, driven by making money, there is a whole class of predatory financial companies who take over profitable firms to strip their assets. It is perfectly legitimate for one company to prey on another, for a larger firm to buy up a smaller one (or even a smaller firm to buy a bigger one, if it can raise the finance) and strip out its best assets then close it down. A larger company can temporarily lower its prices to put smaller rivals out of business.

The vagaries of the financial markets means that a business deal that spans several countries with different currencies may be socially valuable and profitable when set up. It can suddenly become unprofitable due to changes in conversion rates of currencies, or because there is a new entry into the market where wages are lower or environmental regulation is looser. These are events that have no relation to social and environmental benefits but effect the continued viability of an organisation.

In a money-driven economy, activities may be destructive yet profitable, so companies will defend them against criticism, as for example, the tobacco industry running publicity campaigns saying smoking is safe, or the oil companies funding the climate change denial campaigns, or arguing for the use of pesticides that are killing bees. Dangers are harder to catch if they are money making. By contrast the co-operative economy is driven by the health of the real economy.

A co-operative economy is very much more efficient than competitive markets

We are very used to propaganda that says that the competitive market is the most efficient way of running an economy, especially compared to supposedly inefficient, and potentially corrupt government-run services. Actually, it is grossly inefficient in real terms, meaning serving the community with the best use of material and human resources.

Chapter 12 A sustainable Earth described how a co-operative economy could be organised to be much more efficient: local production to reduce transport needed, products that are designed to last a long time, to be repaired, reused, and recycled, so much less production is needed.

In a market where all are competing against each other, it doesn't make sense for one group to give their best ideas to another, even if both are co-operatives. On the contrary, it makes sense for them to stop anyone else using them, as happens now. On the other hand, in a co-operative economy, sharing best practice makes obvious sense.

The ability to share best practice is just the first crack in the idea that markets are efficient ways to provide our needs. The next big step is to realise how much effort (in terms of resources and people) is consumed directly and indirectly by competition. The well-known Quaker two mules

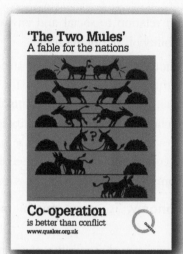

poster makes the basic idea clear. The mules are spending most of their effort pulling against each other until they realise that they can work together.

The size of the conflict-related industries, the 'military-industrial complex' is only the starting point. In an economy driven by money, the interests of the consumer and producer are opposed.

In the conventional economy, most people need to work in order to be able to consume. (There are many exceptions: inherited wealth, income from investments, fees and royalties from earlier work, income from crime.) Production becomes desirable and necessary for its own sake, so long as it can bring in money. There is no natural limit to the amount of money you can have, and thus no limit to the desirable amount of production.

In the conventional economy it is sensible for a producer to use advertising to convince people to want their products, to distort needs and wants in their favour. If you can convince people to buy your product because it is fashionable or because you can prey on their insecurities, your business will do well. If you can convince people to buy shoddy goods without them realising it, you might become rich.

In a co-operative economy driven by wellbeing, there is no need to spend effort on advertising to encourage people to consume. In an economy that isn't dominated by finance (as sketched in the Pinecone Partnership story in

Chapter 3) most of people's material and social needs are met by their communities. There is little or no need for insurance, banks, pensions, taxes, cash, cashiers or cash registers, accountants, stock markets, futures markets, money markets, no negotiations over prices and wages.

>**You**: There are lots of jobs tied up in those activities. Are you saying they would be abolished?

>**Me**: Not abolished, just not needed or hardly needed. The point is that there would be a lot less work needed to produce a reasonable life for people. That is part of what I mean by the vastly greater efficiency of a co-operative economy, and see below for more. As for the implicit issue in your question, of unemployment, the answer in a collaborative economy is simply to share whatever workload there is. If it is lower, there is less to do for everyone.

By contrast, there is a lot of effort spent on finding out what people want and how satisfied they are with what they have received. There is a lot of effort spent on determining the real costs of consumption and informing people of it.

There is no longer a conflict between efficiency and the producer's need to sell more. This was clear in the way computers and automobiles were handled in Pinecone Partnership. Far less has to be produced if the goal is to satisfy people's desires directly than needs to be produced to fuel endless economic growth.

Finally, in a co-operative economy the money-related motivations for crime and corruption are largely removed. Moreover, a social structure like that of a Pinecone Partnership inherently takes into account the diversity of people's Views, so much less conflict occurs. This leads to a much lower workload for police and social services.

A co-operative economy, driven directly by the needs of people and the environment, (the third basic eGaian principle) has the possibility of being a society that works in accordance with people's hopes and dreams. It has the possibility of being a healthy society, in which the Global Cancer has been cured.

PART 4
MAKING EGAIA
HAPPEN

14 Starting points

"New forms of society are possible and practical. They are the indispensable pathway to the creation of a new planetary balance in social, economic, human and cultural terms."[145]

The eGaian vision we have been exploring may be very far from mainstream, as presented in the media or by politicians, but the good news is that there are huge numbers of people, projects and organisations all around the world that are working towards parts or all of it. There are also major social trends, such as our connections to each other online and through social media, that are consistent with the vision and pre-adapt our society to it.

---

[145] From *"Constitutzione della Federazione di Damanhur"*, Damanhur, 1999 (in 4 languages), p.157.

In her classic book, *The Aquarian Conspiracy*,[146] Marilyn Ferguson chronicled many of those starting points, as they appeared 30 years ago:

"The paradigm of the Aquarian Conspiracy sees humankind embedded in nature. It promotes the autonomous individual in a decentralised society. It sees us as stewards of all our resources, inner and outer. It says that we are not victims, not pawns, not limited by conditions or conditioning. Heirs to evolutionary riches, we are capable of imagination, invention, and experiences we have only glimpsed."

The website wiser.org (now no longer active) was the modern equivalent to Ferguson's book and listed over one hundred thousand relevant organisations.

It is easy to be pessimistic if you only encounter mainstream media. The twentieth century saw the development of the global cancer to its most destructive limits with globalisation, but at the same time, it brought with it the possibility of global-scale coherence.

Could it be that the progression to planetary-scale coherence has happened many times before elsewhere in the universe? And perhaps a common part of that process is that as life becomes increasingly complex it takes its planet to the very edge of destruction before it makes that final leap to unity?

If the Earth is to achieve a global-scale coherence, it will need:

- a communication system linking the various parts, leading to
- symbiosis among the parts, so that they act in aid of each other and the whole rather than in conflict and competition with each other, leading to
- a global sense of identity, people seeing themselves as people of the Earth, looking after each other and the natural world.

This chapter looks at recent and current starting points towards these three features, including a review of some of the organisations whose work is heading in that direction.

---

[146] Marilyn Ferguson, *The Aquarian Conspiracy, Personal and Social Transformation in the 1980s*, Tarcher, 1980.

A COMMUNICATION SYSTEM

Communication has been a human strong point since the early stages of our evolution as 'the co-operative ape' when we developed language. Travel has given humans glimpses of cultures other than their own since ancient times. Conquests and migrations have long led to the mixing of cultures and languages. But only with the development of electronic communications in the last 100 years has our communication reached the stage where it could be the basis of a global nervous system.

The transition started in the late 19th century, with the invention of the telegraph and telephone, especially when undersea cables linked the continents. In the early 20th century, motion pictures and then radio linked the world much more closely. In the mid-20th century, with TV news sent by satellite, wars, famines and other crises became much more visible in homes around the world. Air travel became more widely available. With so much travel and the globalisation of business, English began to emerge as the first global language, spoken by at least some people everywhere.

But it was the end of the 20th century, with the development of mobile telephones and the mass use of the Internet that provided the necessary infrastructure for a global nervous system. It now pervades the world. Even developing countries have rapidly growing Internet access, with access points in many small towns and even villages. Across the world, some 2.4 billion people were on-line by 2012.[147] This is an increase by a factor of about 5 since 2000 (and since the first publication of this book) and is nearly one third of the world's population.

Social networks are now ubiquitous and have been said to have triggered mass social movements such as Occupy and the Arab Spring.

> **You** Are you saying that the Internet is the global nervous system?
>
> **Me** No, it's not the Internet itself. That only provides the infrastructure. It is the way people are coming to use it, and could use it in the future, which might provide the global

---

[147] http://www.internetworldstats.com/stats.htm

nervous system. The change has been so dramatic within my lifetime. When I was a child, my grandparents immigrated to New York by ship, and air travel was a luxury. A long distance telephone call (to the one phone in the house!) was a rare and exciting event. Now, our children travel to distant places and we worry if they don't text us or email us from a cyber-café every few days. Friends with young children casually check up on them during the day, mobile phone to mobile phone. But this is only connection. It is the use of that connection to provide mutual support and co-ordination that could make a global nervous system.

SYMBIOSIS AMONG THE PARTS

The growth in a sense of the connectedness of all humanity has lead to many initiatives and to the creation of many organisations dedicated to resolving the world's problems. At present their influence is very much smaller than that of the global cancer but it is growing rapidly.

For example, the past few decades have seen a huge increase of non-governmental organisations (NGOs) which are neither commercial organisations nor governmental. Although they do not have much power, they have increasing influence, through very large numbers of supporters and good means of communications. They range from think tanks that propose policies and lobby governments to grassroots organisations taking direct action.

There are several million(!) NGOs in the world[148], and they have become a new force in world governance, taking on a global role where governments are unable to.

"A living body of networking organizations has emerged to fill the niche produced by dysfunctional post-colonial governments. A plethora of unique interdependent organs assuming specialised functions which serve the whole have almost magically become the body that promises better life for the people in developing countries, and the whole Earth.

Grassroots Organizations (GROs) formed by the people in remote villages, have risen by the tens of thousand to solve local problems with local skills and local resources. They network horizontally with one another to provide mutual aid. Grassroots Support Organizations (GRSOs) have emerged independently in the cities, capitals and universities to answer their own need for social usefulness by providing information, material and services, to the remote and the disadvantaged GROs.

Overseas International NonGovernmental Organizations (INGOs) have recognized the failure of Governments and UN-run Development Decades to provide "direct aid" to the people in their villages. This whole global Civil Society is a new phenomenon. It was not planned by the bureaucrats, not even by the participants themselves. It emerged and self-organized as a working whole within the last two decades. It is now

---

[148] See the Wikipedia article on nongovernmental organisations.

composed of hundreds of thousands of new organizations each playing a unique role in the new body politic."[149]

A GLOBAL SENSE OF IDENTITY

The enormous growth of communications and mutual support has lead to the beginnings (and we are still at a very early stage) of a global sense of identity. Mainstream politicians still talk about 'doing better than our competitors' meaning people in other countries who are 'other' not 'us'. At the same time, growing numbers of people are coming to identify themselves as 'people of the Earth', empathising with the trials and sufferings of people on the other side of the world. To such people no-one is 'other'.

The availability of comparatively cheap long-distance transport has led to a world that is much more multi-cultural and much more culturally convergent. Small communities of foreigners are now much more common throughout the world, partially keeping their own languages and customs and partially adopting local ways. Food, clothing and consumer goods were once produced locally. Now there are familiar brands bought around the world.

There is, at the same time, a lot of cultural conflict in reaction to immigrant groups and at the same time tolerance and acceptance of different ways of living. The films, television programmes and advertisements of the 1940s and 50s show stereotypes of race and cultural minorities, gender and sexual preference that would be considered intolerable today. Tolerance has the backing of law in many countries and is enshrined in United Nations documents.

The realisation that human affairs are having a significantly harmful effect on the environment entered mass public consciousness only in the 1960s, creating a strong sense that we are all connected on that level at least.

---

149 From a review at http://www.permacult.com.au/community/ngo.html of Julie Fisher, *Nongovernments: NGOs and the Political Development of the Third World*, Kumarian Press, 1997.

There have been various events that have so stirred the global consciousness that they could be called 'eGaian moments'.

- The first views of the Earth from space and the first moonwalks dramatically displayed the whole Earth as a single, closed system containing us all.

- The global aid events of the mid-1980s – Band Aid and Live Aid – showed how universal musical culture was among the young and was a global expression of concern for those people in the most need.

- September 11th was seen live on television – the second plane hitting and the collapse of the twin towers – by millions of people around the world. People were personally shocked by this in a global wave of emotion. Local papers everywhere reported on local people who had been involved. Amazing petitions circulated on the Internet in response, with signatures that leapt from nation to nation. eGaia felt pain and shock.

- Environmental news such as the milestone of reaching a concentration of 400 ppm of carbon dioxide in the atmosphere, or the melting of the Arctic Ice Cap brings home to the whole world that we are now all connected and interdependent.

SOME ORGANISATIONS AND MOVEMENTS TO WATCH

To give you a better sense of the type of activities happening all over the world that are starting points towards an eGaian world, here is a short list of organisations and movements – a quite arbitrary selection from the huge number out there.

The Co-operative and Commons movements

New forms of community enterprise and co-operatives would be at the core of an eGaian world. Taking a long view of human history, this can be seen as a return to the kind of social support that shaped human evolution and to which human minds and personalities are adapted (as discussed in *Chapter 8 The co-operative ape*). In recent history there have been many experiments with co-operatives such as:

216

- the pioneering efforts in the 19th century co-operative movement in Britain;
- the kibbutz movement in Israel;
- the hippie communes and communities in the 1960s and 70s.

While the co-operative movement has radical origins, today it is so commonplace it is hardly noticed. Moreover, in some places, it has been seduced by the mainstream economy and often appears hardly different from privately owned businesses, although its underlying ideology is very different.

The extent of co-operatives around the world is huge, as these figures[150] show:

- 75 % of Fairtrade goods are produced by co-operatives of smallholders.
- Over 1 billion people worldwide are members of co-operatives.
- Over 3 billion people secure their livelihoods through co-operatives.
- Co-operatives employ more than 20% more people than multinational corporations.

Over the past few years, many people with views similar to those in this book[151] have been talking about re-inventing the co-operative movement, and linking it with the environmental movement. Most co-operatives now are either workers' co-operatives, owned and run by their employees, or consumer co-operatives, that combine their purchasing influence so they can somewhat redress the advantage that large private companies have. Now there is talk of 'multi-stakeholder co-ops' that are run for the benefit of all concerned: employees, customers, suppliers and the wider community.[152]

---

[150] From the Co-operatives UK website.

[151] for example, Michael Lewis and Pat Conaty, *The Resilience Imperative, Cooperative Transition to a Steady-State Economy*, New Society, 2012.

[152] Pat Conaty, Social Co-operatives: a Democratic Co-production Agenda for Care Services in the UK, Cooperatives UK, 2013.

A new strand has appeared, talking about commons – resources that once were understood to be for the benefit of all, but have been appropriated for the benefit of a few. The most significant of these is land, such as communal grazing, or water supplies and fisheries. They have been shown to be better managed and more productive through co-operative rather than private ownership and control.[153]

There are some places where co-operatives have moved to the next level, with large numbers working together, supported by a layer of secondary co-ops providing services and co-ordination to them, most notably the Mondragon co-ops in the Basque region of Spain, and the Emilia Romagna province of Italy.

Example: Emilia Romagna[154]: "The experience of Emilia Romagna in northern Italy is a compelling story, because it demonstrates that there is an alternative that not only adheres to the values of a vibrant civil society, but has also transmitted these values to the creation of a highly successful commercial economy.

Emilia Romagna is a region of 3.9 million people situated in the north of Italy, just below the foothills of the Italian Alps. Bologna, the region's most populous city, is the commercial and communications hub of the area, and the home of Europe's oldest university. The *artigianati*, or self employed artisans, account for 41.5% of the companies in the region. Over 90% of these enterprises employ fewer than 50 people. This is typical of the small firms in the area. Indeed, there are only five firms that employ over 500. Two of these, SACMI and CMR, are co-operatives.

Small firms working in co-operative networks within industrial districts are the keys to the Emilian economy. In turn, the principles of co-operation and the adoption of reciprocity and mutual benefit for economic objectives are the philosophical and social bases of the system. No less important is

[153] Elinor Ostrom, *Governing the Commons, The Evolution of Institutions for Collective Action*, Cambridge University Press, 1990.

[154] John Restakis, The Emilian Model: Profile of a Co-operative Economy. Canadian Co-operative Association - BC Region (now BCCA), 2000.

the fact that the policies of the Region government actively promote co-operative relations among firms.

Most public works, including large-scale engineering, construction, and heritage restoration projects, are carried out by building co-operatives owned by their employee members.

Similarly, the region's agricultural co-ops are Europe's leaders in organic food production and environmentally friendly pest control.

The model of co-operative organizations that provide shared services for their members has been applied to research & development, education & training, marketing & distribution, financing, technology transfer, workplace safety, environmental regulation, and a host of other services that help small and medium sized firms to compete in a global marketplace.

What all these centres have in common is that they replicate the advantages of large corporate structures for the collection and application of global knowledge for production, while maintaining the strengths which are unique to small enterprise.

Another key to the success of these small enterprises is the role of financial consortia which provide ready and inexpensive capital to local firms. Operating like lending circles, individual loans are guaranteed by every other firm in the consortium, and the resulting default rate is a fraction of what it would be for a bank.

All members of the manufacturing network are known to each other, have long standing economic and social relationships, and see themselves as part of an organic, if informal, economic system

Unlike the profit principle which animates the private economy, the reciprocity principle entails a relationship based on trust and mutual exchange and which says, "I will help you now, on the understanding that you will reciprocate later". This is precisely what the co-operating firms do in manufacturing networks. One firm will outsource to other firms on the expectation that those firms will reciprocate to them later. As in a classic co-operative system, the success of one firm is intimately bound up with the success of the others.

As described in Italian legislation, social co-ops have as their purpose "to pursue the general community interest in promoting human concerns and the integration of citizens". In this sense, social co-operatives are recognized as having goals that maximize benefits to the community and its citizens, rather than maximizing profits to co-op members."

The Transition Town movement

The first 'transition town' was started in the small, rural town of Totnes in England by Rob Hopkins in 2006, "as a response to the challenges our community is facing from diminishing oil and gas supplies, coupled with climate change and economic uncertainty.[155]" The kind of 'responses' they created were practical, on-the-ground community projects covering local food, transport, energy, community spirit, housing and more. That is, they were working to create solutions themselves, at a community level, rather than protesting, complaining, or asking their government to act differently.

Probably the biggest appeal of the transition movement is that it is hugely empowering to the people involved. They don't have to stand by hopelessly while the global cancer moves inexorable onwards. They feel they can take matters in their own hands, in their own communities, and start to live differently.

This approach quickly found a wide appeal to people first in other towns nearby, then further afield in the United Kingdom, and more recently around the world. In September 2013 there were nearly 500 'official' transition towns (referred to as 'transition initiatives') listed on their website, on every continent, and over one thousand including what they call 'mullers', or groups that are starting out but haven't yet been officially recognised.

As the number of transition towns began to grew, its founders set up a charity, the Transition Network, in 2009, to support them. The Transition

---

155 http://www.transitiontowntotnes.org/about/

Network has produced various books, short films, trainings, and other materials, to help local initiatives, and has held regular conferences. It has grown and has attracted lots of funding from a range of foundations, some of whom are saying, in effect, "we can see there are major problems, and you are some of the only people with a practical solution."

The transition town movement is not dogmatic, promoting just one strategy. It is experimental and exploratory, inviting people to find the solutions that best suit their own communities. It offers a 'cheerful disclaimer':

> "Just in case you were under the impression that Transition is a process defined by people who have all the answers, you need to be aware of a key fact. We truly don't know if this will work. Transition is a social experiment on a massive scale."

Some of the kinds of projects that transition towns take on are: food growing groups, community-owned bakeries, breweries and energy companies, groups that help people insulate their houses and reduce their daily energy use, local currencies.

Example: Sustainable Bungay[156]: In the East of England is a small town called Bungay with a very active transition group. According to its newsletter, some of its current and recent projects are:

- Happy Mondays: a shared meal of local food open to the community;
- Green Drinks: a regular discussion group over drinks at a local pub;
- Sewing Sundays: a monthly skill share at the local library;
- Local group bicycle rides, and a car free day;
- Bungay Bees: trains people to keep bees;
- Give and Take Days: exchange of unwanted household items;
- An abundance of fruit: collecting and exchange fruit for free;
- Pig Club: group raising of pigs organically;
- Give and Grow: food sharing, plant exchange.

---

[156] http://www.sustainablebungay.com/

Transition projects are seen as collaborative and community-scale, so there is also an emphasis on the skills of working together, building community relationships, understanding each other, handling conflicts constructively, which they refer to as 'inner transition'.

As the number of transition towns has grown, and the international dimension has become more prominent, there has been a growing emphasis on encouraging the local initiatives to work collaboratively as a mutual support system at regional and even national level. There are now regional support groups and various 'national hubs' that have their own conferences. There is the beginning of the 'locally-based but globally connected' approach described in earlier chapters.

> **You** Do I remember you saying that you are active in the Transition Network?

> **Yes** I have been part of this for several years, as it seems to me the nearest I have seen to the vision in this book. I have worked on local projects, a regional network, and had a term on the Transition Network Board of Trustees. If you are looking for a way to participate in creating this vision, my top tip would be to look at the Transition Network website, find and join a transition group near you, or start one if there isn't one already.

Global Ecovillage Network

While the transition towns movement helps people to create a new way of living in their existing communities, 'ecovillages' are a more radical solution: creating entirely new communities that are dedicated to sustainable living. Some of these are internationally known, like Findhorn in Scotland, Auroville in India or Damanhur in Italy.

> "An ecovillage is a human-scale settlement consciously designed through participatory processes to secure long-term sustainability. All four dimensions (the economic, ecological, social and cultural) are seen as mutually reinforcing."[157]

---

[157] http://gen-europe.org/ecovillages/about-ecovillages/index.htm

The Global Ecovillage Network was formed in 1995 following a conference at Findhorn on 'Ecovillages and Sustainable Communities" and has grown rapidly. Its conference in 2013, brought together over 300 people from 51 countries.

"Never have the international connections, mutual support, and love between the ecovillages of the Global South and the Global North been so visible and palpable.[158]"

An ecovillage may be as small as a few families or large communities of hundreds of people, with as much variety in their form as in their size. Many are 'intentional' communities, with a clear purpose that may be spiritual or political, while others are simply groups of people wanting to live in harmony with each other and nature.

The Federation of Damanhur is an example of a large, well-established eco-village, that is quite prominent in the Global Eco-village Network. The group was formed in 1975, encouraged by the teachings of Oberto Airaudi, who was Damanhur's spiritual guide until his death in 2013.

"Damanhur is a collective dream transformed into reality thanks to the creative power of positive thought. It is a laboratory for the future, a seed that has been growing for over thirty years, constantly transforming and renewing itself so as to bring to life the reality its citizens together dreamed of and built.[159]"

In 1979 they inaugurated their first community village. It has developed since then into a federation of communities, largely spread around the Valchiusella valley in the foothills of the Alps north of Turin. It has around 1,000 citizens, most of whom are resident in the communities.

The Earth is seen as a living thing which the people are expected to look after. Damanhurian society is mutually supportive and organism-like rather than competitive. From the beginning it was seen as a spiritual community.

---

[158] http://gen.ecovillage.org/index.php/news/279--gen-conference-7-12-july-2013-celebrating-a-worldwide-movement.html

[159] http://www.damanhur.org/about-us/1252-damanhur-a-laboratory-for-the-future

Communication, conflict resolution and seeing from another's perspective are an important part of Damanhur's educational principles. Where problems do arise they are dealt with informally. On those rare occasions when it is necessary, their 'College of Justice' intervenes using an approach of restorative justice aimed at healing the social breaches rather than punishment, just as suggested in the eGaian Guide.

Economically, the various businesses of Damanhur function as autonomous profit-making enterprises and are generally quite successful. Most of the Damanhur businesses are run as co-operatives by their employees. Although largely autonomous, they are subject to the principles of the Damanhurian philosophy and Constitution. They are not in competition with each other. Rather, each has its own niche and role in Damanhurian society.

One clear lesson from Damanhur is that it is possible to live much more sustainably when you are part of a community that acts as a whole towards sustainable ends than it is for an isolated individual. They have created a co-operative bubble within the larger competitive world. This frees them to move towards sustainable living.

The Permaculture Association

Permaculture is another movement that is spreading around the world, with a philosophy that strongly overlaps with an eGaian approach. There is also a lot of overlap with transition towns, as Rob Hopkins, the founder of transition towns started as a permaculture teacher.

"The word 'permaculture' comes from 'permanent agriculture' and 'permanent culture' - it is about living lightly on the planet, and making sure that we can sustain human activities for many generations to come, in harmony with nature. Permanence is not about everything staying the same. Its about stability, about deepening soils and cleaner water, thriving communities in self-reliant regions, biodiverse agriculture and social justice, peace and abundance.[160]"

---

[160] http://www.permaculture.org.uk/knowledge-base/basics

Permaculture was developed by Bill Mollison and David Holmgren in the 1970s in Australia. It was originally an approach to stable agricultural systems in reaction to industrial agricultural methods, and this is what it is mostly known for. However, it was later broadened to become a design approach for sustainable human settlements.

It is a design philosophy that uses natural systems as a model for agriculture. It includes such elements as the inclusion of perennial crops, agro-forestry, companion cropping, using multiple layers mimicking a forest to maximise productivity, mulching to suppress weeds and build fertility, but especially, careful observation and planning to take advantage of the detailed characteristics of any site.

The Permaculture Association seems to be organised primarily around groups that are learning permaculture principles. The learners then go on to apply it to gardens and farms and other projects. Although there is no formal organisational structure to these groups, there is a lot of communication between them, for social events and mutual support. In the UK, the Permaculture Association is trying to apply viable systems principles to improve their organisation.

The new economy and the gift economy

As global markets create more and more problems throughout the world, many alternatives and experiments have arisen in reaction to it. The ethical investment movement allows people to put their savings into banks and investment funds that have criteria other than maximising returns. This may mean as little as a stock market fund which avoids armaments and other harmful companies, or as much as the Triodos Bank which specialises in investments in social and environmentally beneficial enterprises. Micro-credit banks specialise in making very small loans to people in developing countries or deprived neighbourhoods in the West. These people would normally be unable to obtain any credit at all.

Many organisations and individuals have been analysing what is wrong, propose solutions and develop projects. Here are some that are more or less consistent with the analysis in earlier chapters.

225

New Economics Foundation (London)

"The new economics foundation is an independent think-and-do tank that inspires and demonstrates real economic wellbeing."

and the New Economics Institute (Cambridge, MA, USA)

"The mission of the New Economics Institute is to build a New Economy that prioritizes the wellbeing of people and the planet."

These are two sister organisations that are researching the problems with our economy and running projects to prototype solutions. For example

Stakeholder Banks: "co-operative banks, credit unions, community development finance institutions (CDFIs), and public interest savings banks. Their common characteristic is the goal of creating value for stakeholders, not just shareholders."

Community Currencies: "These community-led, bottom-up exchange systems stimulate more vibrant, equitable and sustainable economies locally. We researched and worked with LETS, timebanking, the Brixton and Bristol Pounds, and support innovation and implementations of currency initiatives in the EU-Interreg project Community Currencies in Action."

"*Key Facts*

- The Swiss WIR complementary currency has an annual turnover of 1.2 billion Swiss Francs, serving 62,000 SMEs and has been existence since 1934

- The Brixton Pound has now registered over 1000 pay-by-text users

- Supported by the Central Bank, the Brazilian Banco Palmas currency and community bank has been replicated over 100 times."

Positive Money is an organisation that campaigns for monetary reform. They produce very clever videos that explain how the money system works, especially the idea that money is created by banks making loans, and the problems this creates. If you want to be clearer about how this creates the need for economic growth and how it funnels money to the already wealthy, look at their website. Their principal remedy is for money creation to be taken away from banks and given to governments.

All three of these organisations are very critical of our money system, especially as compared with the uncritical acceptance of the financial and government establishments. Going beyond this, there are people and groups talking about 'gift economies'.

An important champion of the gift economy is Charles Eisenstein, a writer and speaker whose starting point is the sense of separation between people, and the coming change to a broader sense of identity, very much like the eGaian image.

His book Sacred Economics...

> "traces the history of money from ancient gift economies to modern capitalism, revealing how the money system has contributed to alienation, competition, and scarcity, destroyed community, and necessitated endless growth. Today, these trends have reached their extreme – but in the wake of their collapse, we may find great opportunity to transition to a more connected, ecological, and sustainable way of being.

This book is about how the money system will have to change—and is already changing—to embody this transition. A broadly integrated synthesis of theory, policy, and practice, Sacred Economics explores avant-garde concepts of the New Economics, including negative-interest currencies, local currencies, resource-based economics, gift economies, and the restoration of the commons."

The Fair Trade Federation (FTF) is

"an association of fair trade wholesalers, retailers, and producers whose members are committed to providing fair wages and good employment opportunities to economically disadvantaged artisans and farmers worldwide.

FTF directly links low-income producers with consumer markets, and educates consumers about the importance of purchasing fairly traded products which support living wages and safe and healthy conditions for workers in the developing world. It also acts as a clearinghouse for information on fair trade and provides resources and networking opportunities for its members. By adhering to social criteria and environmental principles, Fair Trade Organizations (FTOs) foster a more equitable and sustainable system of production and trade that benefits people and their communities."

AND LOTS MORE...

The above people and projects are just a short and quite random selection of starting points towards the vision in this book. Major omissions certainly include the global search for peace, inner personal development and many spiritual movements. The big question is whether and how they might move from being the concern of a small proportion of humanity to being mainstream. That will be the concern of the next chapter.

15 The next big step(s)?

"If humanity were to evolve into a healthy, integrated social super-organism, it would signal the maturation and awakening of the global nervous system."
Peter Russell

This chapter looks to the future, building upon the starting points in the last chapter. What might be the next big steps that would take the starting points to the next level, where they are no longer quite so marginal and might begin a take-off to becoming mainstream?

You I thought you said that wouldn't happen until there is a crash?

Me Yes, I think it isn't likely that this vision will become mainstream, meaning, accepted by a large part of the population, before a financial crash. But I do think it could become much less marginal in the lives of people who already share much of the vision, such as those who are active in the starting points. Also there are growing numbers of people who are in severe financial difficulties, for whom the crash is happening now, and they may be receptive to these ideas. What is important is that there are enough examples of the new co-operative vision so that it will take off when there is a crash.

The key change for this moment in time is the joining up of these starting points, so that they are connected with each other, aware of each other's activities and start searching for synergies. In what practical, day to day ways can they help each other?

It doesn't need to be everyone active in these groups who do this, just a few, who come to see how they can begin to work first with similar groups, and then with others that share a similar world view.

You This sounds like the metamorphosis of the caterpillar to the butterfly you talked about in the introductory chapter, where the imaginal disks begin to join up.

229

Yes Exactly so. The big idea is that there while there are many ways of working towards this vision, they will all eventually be small parts of a single whole, humanity working to look after itself and the natural world. There is only one co-operative economy, one movement towards mutual understanding and peace, not a lot of little ones in competition with each other. And there are lots of people who see this as the next big step.

Many people are proposing projects and activities with the aim of bringing together many diverse projects and groups. The idea that now is the time for the diverse strands of this loose movement to join is gaining popularity. There are 'networks of networks', moves to join the environmental movement with the co-operatives and commons movements, and a range of educational projects, among many.

AN EGAIAN EXCHANGE NETWORK

Me: I'm really going to stick my neck out in this section and concentrate on just one approach. This is my favourite idea that I think could really make all the difference to bringing a collaborative world into the mainstream.

You: So this is your pet idea.

Me: Yes it is. In the first edition of eGaia I called these 'eGaian community networks'. Having tried hard to set these up since then, I now see how hard it is and how far even from the starting points in the last chapter. This time around I'll break it up into separate steps that could be started one at a time, or combined to form something a lot more powerful.

It is an attempt to re-invent community, actually to create a new social contract, and to do so in a way that enables people to lead lives that are more sustainable and co-operative. It provides starting points for an economy based upon trust, where the pressures of the commercial marketplace are significantly reduced. It builds on the ideas behind eco-villages but without requiring people to give up their existing homes and livelihoods and move to a new community. It builds on transition towns, using social networks to add much more co-ordination and a major economic dimension.

Essentially, these are starting points to the system of exchange in the *'Taste of an eGaian future'* chapter. It takes people that are sympathetic to the collaborative world view and makes it easy for them to find ways to work together for mutual benefit. It combines new forms of money and gift economy with an organised local exchange.

The success of an exchange will depend upon whether it offers its members immediate, personal benefits, and must be set up with that in mind. Particularly in the early stages, their larger effects on the world will be extremely small and must be secondary.

Step 1 Recruitment: Becoming explicit about who is part of this

Can we simply encourage people to identify publicly with the essence of this vision? We would hope to attract people across many different movements and projects, who might be willing to accept some common vision and would appreciate contact with people who would be willing to help each other in various ways.

Perhaps it can be explicit about being part of a 'global family that looks after people and the Earth' or just 'People Care, Earth Care' or some other metaphor that might be widely accepted?

That means people who don't see themselves as competing with everyone else, who are hoping to live in modest comfort rather than to earn as much money as possible, and who care about the state of the natural world.

This need not be limited to people who are currently active in the starting points, but also include people who are looking for ways out of the current system, at least in part, and especially businesses and organisations who want to be part of it.

It would give all of them a tremendous lift, a sense that they are not struggling on their own, but are part of a rapidly-growing, global movement.

A major side effect of this would be to establish the idea that there are real, viable alternatives to our social and economic systems – a view that is almost totally absent in the media and political debates.

To do this would probably require identifying a small set of broad principles that characterise it. Then people, organisations, businesses can sign up to them, perhaps on one or more suitable websites. Here's a first try at this:

Joining the 'global family that looks after people and the Earth' means:

- *Relationships*: Agreeing to treat all people with respect, acting with integrity. This includes a commitment to handle any disagreements or conflicts that arise constructively.

- *Environment*: Appreciating the environmental challenges we are facing, attempting to align our personal lives and business dealings with best environmental practice.

- *Money as servant, not as master:* Financial transparency and integrity: giving priority to the wellbeing of people and the natural world over maximising money. This includes a commitment to paying fair and ethical prices and wages, rather than looking for the lowest price or highest salary. It also requires a transparency over profits, wages and salaries, so it is clear that these are neither excessive nor exploitative.

Step 2 Informal mutual support and gift exchange

With these people/organisations/businesses known to each other, perhaps listed on some suitable websites, and with their agreed statement of principles, this recruitment could be seen as creating a market and a basis for exchanging gifts and favours. People and businesses who are part of it should then see the others in it as people they would wish to preferentially buy from, sell to, employ, or give and receive support from. It is a recruitment to an ethical, environmentally-minded sector within the open market.

As a starting point, most people who declare themselves in this way will find lots of their friends and others in their area who they are already doing favours for, buying and selling from, etc. so this step would initially just be doing more of what they are already doing.

These lists would include the many businesses that are known for their personal service, integrity and for their environmental concern. They would be promoted to like-minded people, creating the beginnings of a market that is driven by service, not profit.

Another dimension of this is for similar projects to look for ways to support each other. For example, community farms and permaculture projects could share tools and expertise, provide labour for each other when needed, help each other's organisations when they are struggling.

> **You** Let me be clear about this. You aren't saying 'we need to overthrow the old system' you are saying 'invite sympathetic people to grow a new economy within the old'.
>
> **Me** Exactly so.

At this stage, a key part of the communication process would be regular social and cultural events to establish and strengthen relationships.

> **You** So this emerging movement might be known for its great parties!
>
> **Me** Yes, exactly. But perhaps they would be parties at which people were also checking out what each others' needs were and how they might help each other: favours, gifts, buying, selling, hiring each other, ways of helping each other to need less money.

Step 3 Creating more formal mutual support mechanisms

Once there are identified people and businesses in an area who recognise each other as part of the 'global family' and who are looking for ways to support each other, there is a context for setting up more organised and formal systems. Here are some of them, as described in the 'organising principles for a co-operative economy' in Chapter 13:

> **Me** I am not really clear in what order to put these, so I have lumped them all under step 3.

Specialised websites and apps: The 'Global Family App'

Imagine that for many of your everyday needs you could easily find a local individual or business or community organisation that you know is part of this explicit 'global family looking after people and planet'. These are people you can trust, that you know are doing their best for the environment, and that deal with people with respect and integrity. You might use an app on your phone/tablet/laptop to find them, or to make daily transactions easy.

To support the relationship of trust, the app shows you a list of previous transactions by that person, with you and other people, with ratings and reviews of them by other people you know and trust. Even if they are not that local and you don't know them personally, there is a short chain of friends of friends of friends linking them to you.

As there is a major environmental dimension to this, people making offers would be expected to make some statement of their environmental awareness and performance, and be open to review on this.

If people are preferentially patronising others within the group, then much of the money in use will be recirculating within it.

For people who are open to a gift economy approach, it could have a section for exchange of favours, help given without payment, but within the group where all are giving and receiving. This would be a more formalised system of gift giving than we are used to now for birthdays, Christmas, weddings, etc. with exchanges recorded on the app, and with the possibilities of ratings and reviews.

When an exchange occurs, someone does something for you, or gives you something, this is recorded on both party's profiles and is part of their public record. Thus before you offer a gift or a favour you can look at the receiver's record to get a general idea as to whether they are keeping their giving and receiving roughly in balance or are free-loading.

> **You** I'm not so sure I want all the things I do for my friends listed on some public website.
>
> **Me** I agree. I think people would choose to list actions that weren't too personal or private, especially things that they do for the community. So many people now do volunteer work and get no recognition for it.

234

New forms of 'money' that aren't legal tender

Another approach which might appeal to some people is to avoid the conventional money system, at least for some transactions, with a complementary currency. As in 'Chapter 3 A taste of an eGaian future', this could be a strictly local currency, or it could a global complementary currency, (the 'Eco'?) deployed by some suitable organisation (perhaps a large social or environmental NGO?). It might be built into the 'Global Family App' for ease of use and to keep overheads low.

The NGO would set up the system for global use, but people could use it locally or more widely, if they were clear by other means (i.e. the chain of friends, or the ratings and reviews) that the users were worthy of trust.

It would probably best be denominated in hours, but would be flexible so that people could charge more or less than one Eco for an hour's work, depending upon circumstances. This creates the expectation that everyone's effort is equally worthy of respect, but that there can still be differences, for example, because some work is easy while some is much harder.

This would best be a mutual credit system where money is created and removed through each transaction. It would have credit limits, and fees based upon system costs rather than interest.

These new complementary currencies would be specifically for use by people and organisations who have signed up to the Global Family, to facilitate exchange within it. Thus it would explicitly not be 'legal tender', which has to be accepted by anyone, as is conventional money. Rather, it would be understood to be used only with trusted people and organisations with shared values. Thus it would be backed by the reputations and relationships of its users, and would not need to be convertible into national currency or backed by anything physical.

Organising 'autonomy with coordination' at various scales

By this stage we have a defined group of people with shared values that are committed to supporting each other and the planet, and the beginnings of mechanisms to help them do that. However, there is still the danger that they will see each other as in competition with each other in a specialised market, even though it may be more ethical. Bringing in the 'autonomy with coordination' principles[161] described in Chapter 13 can help them to function more effectively and synergistically.

We are very used to local exchanges or markets where people put up lists of what they offer and what they want, either as classified ads, or even for free using such systems as Freecycle or Freegle. Most complementary currency systems include them too, but the standard criticisms of early complementary currency systems was that 'they were great if you wanted a massage but not if you wanted a plumber'. People would often struggle to find skills that they could offer.

That is because the conventional model of a local exchange is that of a market where people are not connected to each other. A collaborative exchange, such as that described in the fictional *Tastes of an eGaian Future* in Chapter 3 has more possibilities.

It could be set up with small groups to co-ordinate different areas, such as food, transport, housing, child care, energy, social events, etc. Each of these co-ordinating groups could actively seek people to supply needs in their area and act as agents to connect people who have needs with those who could supply those needs. Where extra help was needed, they could advertise that need: "Drivers needed for Saturday evening..., More people needed on Mondays at the Community Farm...," In this way, people looking for ways to serve the community would always be able to find an opportunity. In effect, it would be creating a large number of short, part-time jobs chosen to suit a member's interests and free time. Signing up for these on-line is much easier than the normal hassles of arranging a part-time job.

Beyond that, the co-ordinating groups could help the people they are working with to function more collaboratively using the 'autonomy with collaboration' principles: stability, optimisation, adaptation, policy and identity, as described in chapter 13. So, for example, where people or

---

[161] More commonly described as viable systems principles.

businesses were offering similar services, the co-ordinating group might help them find ways to provide slightly differing offerings, so they appealed to different customers, and to find ways of working with each other when needed, if they were short staffed or overloaded. The objective would be for each to have a stable and sufficient clientele, not to expand at the expense of each other.

One aspect of this co-ordination that is crucial to making this vision work is an effective method of handling conflicts (part of the 'stability' principle). Conflicts always occur in community groups and are one of the most common reasons they fail. At present, there is often no organised or expected way of handling conflicts in groups. It isn't a normal part of most cultures. And worst, there isn't much pressure on people to find a constructive solution. If both parties to a conflict genuinely seek a way through, it is usually possible to find one. If one or both aren't interested, it is very difficult.

Thus a vital part of building a resilient community exchange is to build in the expectation that conflict will be handled constructively. It needs to be part of the rules for joining, one of the values expected of members. In fact, it is one major reason why some kind of membership commitment is likely to be needed. This would then be supported by an agreed procedure to follow if those concerned weren't able to come to agreement by themselves. A small group of trained conflict handlers would be needed.

16 Summary: Towards an eGaian Earth

All that remains now is to tie up all the chapters above with a short summary and conclusion.

Part I From global cancer to global nervous system set the scene for the rest of the book, with a fictional vision of what a collaborative future could look like, a society organised from childhood onwards to help people work well together and to live modestly comfortable lives in harmony with the natural world. This 'Taste of an eGaian Future' was then used throughout the book. It was used to contrast with a description of the problems with our present society as a global cancer: how we are reaching the limits of the Earth, changing the climate, exterminating species, destroying soil, air and water, and then especially, how people aren't even living well at the expense of the Earth, highlighting the central role in that cancer played by our current economic system which creates inequality, inequity, and encourages crime, corruption and wars. It was used in later parts of the book to illuminate the more abstract descriptions of a sustainable and collaborative society.

Part 2 The five billion year story gave the context for visions in the book. It showed that competition and conflict is not the principal basis of the functioning of the natural world, nor the primary driver of evolution. Rather it is the interplay of symbiosis and competition, where in 'survival of the fittest' fitness is understood as symbiosis (as in how well pieces of a puzzle fit together), not a generalised superiority, and competition sharpens the fit.

Similarly, competition is not at the heart of human nature. We evolved as the ultimate co-operative ape, with competition becoming increasingly dominant largely in the most recent few thousand years. It traced the development of humanity as a global cancer over that recent period, as a growing disconnection from each other and from the natural world. This was to make it clear that solutions like 'get rid of capitalism' or 'money should return to the gold standard' are relatively superficial and miss the point.

Part 3 An eGaian guide: philosophy and principles gave a detailed description of the principles of an eGaian world. It started by looking at relationships on a spectrum from fragmented (where you don't identify with the other person) to coherent (where the other person feels like part of your extended self). It showed how coherent relationships were built upon convergent communication, where people know they have been understood, and gave principles for convergent communication. It then took a detailed look at conflict resolution, including descriptions of a range of techniques for handling conflicts constructively.

From there it built up a picture of what a sustainable society would be like, in terms of sustainable land use and sustainable agriculture, approaches to manufacturing that minimise waste and maximise re-use and recycling, all of which reduce energy use sufficiently that renewable energy sources are easily sufficient.

It then looked at how such a sustainable society could function as a large scale, efficient, collaborative economy. It would use principles of 'autonomy with co-ordination' using local decision-making, not hierarchies or centralised control. It would use information systems to provide much of the function of money, and use money in ways that supported exchange between people without dominating it.

Finally, ***Part 4 Making eGaia happen***, looked at the starting points towards an eGaian world: the ways in which our information systems are connecting us in ways that make a global collaborative society possible and plausible; it traced the beginnings of a global sense of identity; and then described just a few of the many existing organisations and movements that are leading towards this sense of identity, and provide opportunities for people who want to work towards it.

It speculated on next major steps, ways in which the starting points could begin to come together to become much more significant. And finally, it described in more detail the next steps that could lead to a community

239

exchange such as described in the fictional *Taste of an eGaian future* story and the *Co-operative Economy* chapter.

Me If you have followed this book so far, I hope you will now see why I am optimistic that the global cancer will not inevitably lead to a destruction of human society and the natural world, and that a global society organised along eGaian lines is already in an embryonic form, and has the prospect of becoming mainstream, if conditions favour it.

I am continually meeting like-minded people, who are working hard for this to happen. A few big steps further, and we will see the emergence of an embryonic, unified global network of people working for the benefit of all humanity and the natural world. The metaphors of a global family, or an emerging nervous system for a living planet will be very appropriate. We will see the emergence of global-scale coherence and co-ordination that are analogous to a planetary-scale being on Earth.